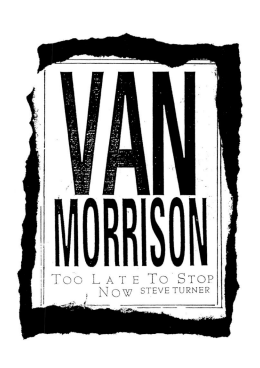

VAN MORRISON

Too Late To Stop Now STEVE TURNER

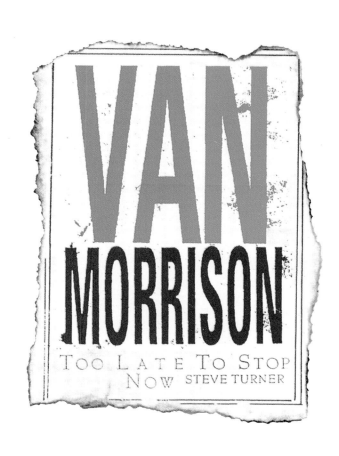

VIKING

VIKING
Published by the Penguin Group
Penguin Books USA Inc., 375 Hudson Street,
New York, New York 10014, U.S.A.
Penguin Books Ltd, 27 Wrights Lane,
London W8 5TZ, England
Penguin Books Australia Ltd, Ringwood,
Victoria, Australia
Penguin Books Canada Ltd, 10 Alcorn Avenue,
Toronto, Ontario, Canada M4V 3B2
Penguin Books (N.Z.) Ltd, 182–190 Wairau Road,
Auckland 10, New Zealand

Penguin Books Ltd, Registered Offices:
Harmondsworth, Middlesex, England

First published in 1993 by Viking Penguin,
a division of Penguin Books USA Inc.

10 9 8 7 6 5 4 3 2 1

Published simultaneously in Great Britain by
Bloomsbury Publishing Limited.

LIBRARY OF CONGRESS
CATALOGING-IN-PUBLICATION DATA
Turner, Steve.
Van Morrison: too late to stop now/Steve Turner.
p.   cm.
ISBN 0–670–85147–7
1. Morrison, Van, 1945– . 2. Singers—Biography. I. Title.
ML420.M63T87   1993
782.42164'092—dc20   93—8286

Design and picture editing by Simon Jennings, Inklink
Typeset by Hewer Text Composition Services, Edinburgh
Printed in the USA by R. R. Donnelley & Sons Company

ACKNOWLEDGEMENTS

IN RESEARCHING THIS BOOK I used the resources of the National Newspaper Library, National Sound Archives, American Federation of Musicians, Decca Records Archives, San Rafael Chamber of Commerce, Wrekin Trust, Polydor Press Office and Sony Music/Legacy Recordings.

I received invaluable help from Amy Herot at Sony Music (New York), Stephen McGinn of the *Van Morrison Newsletter*, Jerry Pompili of Bill Graham Presents (San Francisco), Martin Birlison and Rebecca Fitzgerald at Polydor (London) and Van fan Bob Kennedy, Mick Brown of the *Sunday Telegraph* and Rob Braniff of the Belfast Blues Appreciation Society.

Interviews were carried out with Herbie Armstrong, Jim Armstrong, Brooks Arthur, Eric Bell, Eileen Berns, Graham Blackburn, Ethel Blakely, Walter Blakely, Paul Charles, Bill Dunn, David Hammond, Tommy Hanna, Billy Harrison, Alan Henderson, Chris Hodgkins, Boots Houston, Gil Irvine, Roy Kane, Tom Kielbania, Dougie Knight, Malcolm Lazarus, Solly Lipsitz, Billy McAllen, Nancy McCarter, George McDowell, John Payne, Stephen Pillster, John Platania, Pat Rossi, Mervyn Solomon, Phil Solomon and Eric Wrixon.

My own previously unpublished interview with Van Morrison was taped on 13th December 1985 in Holland Park, London.

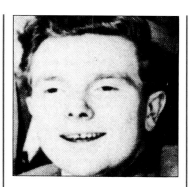

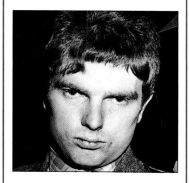

CONTENTS

Van met bluesman John Lee Hooker in the mid-sixties after having been an admirer of his records. They subsequently guested on each other's shows and played on each other's records. In the 1970s Van sang and played guitar on two Hooker album tracks – "Never Get Out of These Blues Alive" and "Goin' Down" – while Hooker recorded a version of Van's song "TB Sheets". In 1993 the two were to join forces on a re-recording of Them's classic song "Gloria", which became a hit in Britain. The two musicians are pictured here in 1989 playing at the end of a jetty beside a Louisiana bayou during a film shoot.

"Above all, it is necessary that the lyric poet's life be known, that we should understand that his poetry is no rootless flower but the speech of a man . . ."
WILLIAM BUTLER YEATS

"I believe that an artist does not belong to the public but to himself. I don't want anyone to know anything about my personal life because it is my personal life to do with what I wish, like anyone else. When a working man comes home on Friday night, what he does Saturday and Sunday is nobody's business but his own."
GEORGE IVAN MORRISON

INTRODUCTION

VAN MORRISON IS A fiercely private individual who only reluctantly consents to interviews. His opinion is that it's enough for the public to have his music, why should they want any more? But this overlooks the fact that a major part of his appeal is the highly autobiographical nature of his work. Few other performers have given us so much detail of where they have come from and what they are going through. And so it would seem reasonable to expect his listeners, especially those who have been captivated by his story because it mirrors their own, to want to know more.

But getting more information does not have to be prurient or obsessive. A fuller understanding of an artist's life, although not essential to the aesthetic experience, can enhance our appreciation. Van Morrison himself is a great devourer of books. In his song "On Hyndford Street" he specifically mentions reading the autobiography *Mr Jelly Roll* by Jelly Roll Morton and *Really the Blues* by Mezz Mezzrow. In "Cleaning Windows" he refers to Jack Kerouac's *Dharma Bums*, a slice of Kerouac's life thinly disguised as fiction. What's more, he describes the reading of these books as memorably ecstatic points in his growing-up experience. One can imagine the young Belfast boy feeling himself out of step with his contemporaries, and finding companionship with the characters that strutted their way out of the pages of these volumes.

This book, while not attempting to be the full-scale biography that Van now deserves, is a comprehensive look in both words and pictures at his long career from teenage showband entertainer to middle-aged mystical legend.

I am a long-standing fan of his music and was able to get to know him in 1985, when researching my study of the relationship between rock music and religion, *Hungry for Heaven*.

To my surprise he responded to a written request for an interview by calling me at home late one night, and suggesting that we get together. The result of this was not only a lengthy interview in which he revealed the spiritual background to his music, but a spasmodic friendship conducted over lunchtime meals in Holland Park and Notting Hill.

I was able to use only a few quotes from the 1985 interview in *Hungry for Heaven*, because he featured only as a part of a general chapter on mysticism. With this book I am able to draw on the information much more extensively, because what he gave me was a unique view of his development which helped me understand his motivations.

I've supplemented this material with first-hand observations from over forty people who have known him well. I've spoken to the children who played with him on Hyndford Street, former schoolteachers, neighbours, musicians, agents, business managers, tour managers and writers. I've then looked at the available writing on Van Morrison, not only the unauthorised biographies but the musical criticism, the reviews, the interviews and news stories dating back to 1962.

If Van thought that in being parsimonious with his comments he would quell the speculation of the public, he has been proved wrong. The long periods between major interviews, his stipulation that interviewers should not bring up "the past" or his "private life", and his refusal to play the star game have only served to increase interest.

He is one of a handful of survivors from the sixties (meaning, artists who cut their first records in the 1960s) whose careers continue to fascinate because they're still willing to walk the tightrope. He is one of those who chose to forsake the possibility of mega pop stardom in favour of a long and substantial career based on integrity. In common with contemporaries like Bob Dylan, Robbie Robertson and Neil Young, Van has used the stuff of his life to fuel his art. A new album from any of these performers is not simply a fresh "collection of tunes" (as they used to say back in the days before rock'n'roll), but a report from the battle front, a diary of the soul.

The main aim of this book is to provide a fuller picture of the life that has produced the songs, in the hope that this will lead to a deeper understanding and a greater enjoyment of the music.

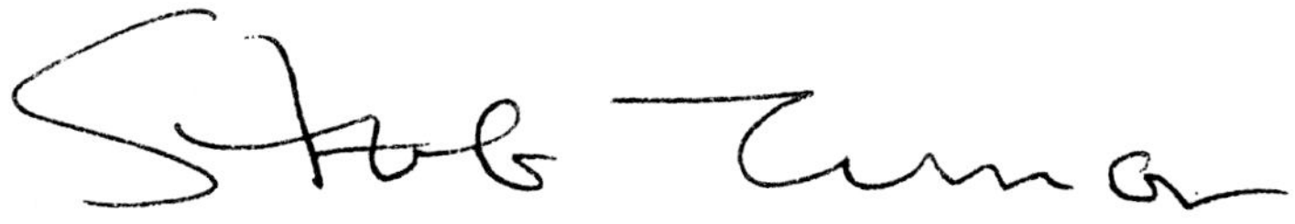

STEVE TURNER

MCMXCIII

The Belfast to which Van continually returns in his songs is the less troubled city captured here in a portrait from the 1950s.

GREENVILLE
ELECTRICAL
SUPPLIES
PHONE 450402
458334

CHAPTER ONE

ON HYNDFORD STREET

Hyndford Street, East Belfast (*left*), was Van's permanent home from 1945 until 1961 and the memory of it continues to inspire his songs. The distant electricity pylon (*right*) provided a meeting place for the boys in the neighbourhood and is mentioned in his song "On Hyndford Street".

VAN MORRISON left Northern Ireland in 1967 and for the next decade appeared to have turned his back on his home country. He paid fleeting visits, but never to perform, the most notable occasion being in March 1974, when he played four concerts in Dublin but none in Belfast. Locals feared that he was avoiding reminders of his humble background in East Belfast. Maybe he'd been spoilt by his mountainside homes in California and upstate New York, and didn't want to return to the city whose name had become a byword for terrorism, strife and violence.

"I'm definitely Irish," he said while living in the splendour of Marin County, "but I don't think I want to go back to Belfast. I don't miss it with all that prejudice around. We're all the same and I think what's happening is terrible."

His attitude was later to soften. After years of tracing his musical heritage to America, he came to believe that blues and soul music owed as much to Scotland and Ireland as they did to Chicago, Memphis and the Mississippi delta. He was a soul singer, yes, but he was a Caledonia soul singer. In 1979 he made his triumphant return to Belfast as a performer at the Whitla Hall, an event that was seen as a symbolic reconciliation between native city and wandering son.

The landscape that informs his songs includes the tree-lined tranquillity of Cyprus Avenue (*top*) and the docks beside the River Lagan. His father once worked at the docks and the sound of the ships' horns, which could be clearly heard on Hyndford Street, recurs in his songs.

During the eighties his visits became more frequent. He looked up old friends, checked out familiar haunts and even bought a house on the coast near Bangor. He seemed to be searching for something of himself that had been lost during the years of exile. In songs like "Irish Heartbeat" and "Celtic Ray" he spoke of responding to the call of his homeland, and of returning to his "own ones".

There had been glimpses of this preoccupation on *Astral Weeks* (1968) when he had referred to his "childlike visions", and the mysteries of being involuntarily "caught up" on Cyprus Avenue, of being "conquered in a car seat". The experiences were beyond words and so he described the landscapes in which they occurred, and they were recognisably those of East Belfast: the old railway track from Cumber to Queens Quay, the ferry boats sailing into the Belfast Lough, the tree-lined sweep of Cyprus Avenue, the looming shapes of the Castlereagh Hills.

Throughout the late sixties and seventies he didn't return to the subject in his songs, but in the eighties, as his interest in his Irish roots developed, he wrote himself back on to the streets of his boyhood. On the albums *No Guru, No Method, No Teacher* in 1986 and *Avalon Sunset* in 1989 he again began to unpack his childhood, now much more conscious of the spiritual implications of his moments of transcendence. Could they have been glimpses of eternity? Had God been tugging on his sleeve?

On *Hymns to the Silence* (1991) he portrayed his days on Hyndford Street as an idyllic period free from fear, confusion and sorrow. As a teenager he had been aware only of cultural constraints and had longed to leave for America. In middle age it had become his Garden of Eden, the place where he had lived before tasting the forbidden fruits of fame and fortune.

Lest we miss the religious significance of this longing, his most explicit request to be taken back to his early days appears in the middle of the old hymn "Just a Closer Walk with Thee". Thus the yearning for the life "way back" on Hyndford Street was paralleled by his prayer for more intimate fellowship with the Lord.

All his forays into fringe religions and delving into esoteric knowledge have formed part of this same quest. He has wanted to recover what has been lost and to discover the source of what he has called his "rapture": "All I was interested in was somewhere to put my experiences and to find out what they were," he once said.

The Bloomfield area of East Belfast seems an unlikely location for mystical experience. It is no Glastonbury or Lourdes, but a working-class district lying between the Castlereagh Hills and the docks on the River Lagan. The landscape is of terraced houses, shopping parades, rubble-strewn wasteground and Victorian factory buildings. There is nothing calculated to uplift the soul, nothing of grandeur or mystery. The religious feeling closest to the surface is that of evangelical Protestantism. Chapels, churches and meeting halls are as widely distributed as pubs in Dublin.

For anyone walking through the streets that Van knew well as a child, it's impossible not to be a Bible reader. From noticeboards the words of Holy Scripture teach, instruct and admonish: "Acquaint now thyself with Him and be at peace," says Grove Baptist Church; "Peace with God through our Lord Jesus Christ," advertises the Shalom Christian Church. They call it the "language of Zion" and Van was to make good use of it in his songs.

Hyndford Street (home to the Bloomfield Gospel Hall where Van sometimes attended Sunday school) is a turning off the Beersbridge Road, and it was here at number 125, a "two up, two down" terraced house with no bathroom, that George Ivan Morrison was born on 31st August 1945. His father was George Morrison, a 25-year-old shipyard worker, and his mother was 24-year-old Violet who had lived at 125 Hyndford Street since she was nine.

George Morrison, who had grown up in nearby Lord Street, had married Violet Stitt on Christmas Day 1941 at St Donard's, the local Church of Ireland on Bloomfield Road whose bells would figure so frequently in their son's songs. On their marriage certificate George was described as an electrician and Violet as a "drawer in a mill".

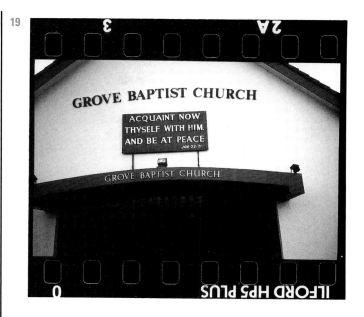

Although Van didn't come from a particularly religious home, the influence of Nonconformism is evident everywhere in East Belfast, and his songs display a familiarity with biblical language. He was born George Ivan Morrison at 125 Hyndford Street.

Although they shared a love of music the two couldn't have been more different in temperament. George was a quiet, shy man who didn't enjoy socialising, whereas Violet was small and vivacious, with a penchant for tap dancing and doing "wee turns" at parties. George Ivan, their only child, was to inherit his father's introverted personality and love of American music, and his mother's instinct for performing.

What distinguished the Morrison family from any other on Hyndford Street was George senior's record collection. At a time when his contemporaries were buying the occasional record by Guy Mitchell or Rosemary Clooney, George senior was acquiring American imports recorded by people with exciting names like Muddy Waters, Howlin' Wolf and Hank Williams. For a Belfast shipyard worker in the late forties such an enthusiasm was considered a sign of eccentricity, and marked George Morrison out as not only quiet and unsociable but odd.

It was while sitting in front of the family gramophone as a child that George Ivan experienced the first of the intense feelings he was later to interpret as a form of spiritual ecstasy. His first memory of this happening dates back to when he was three years old and heard the voice of the American gospel singer Mahalia Jackson. It forged an indelible link in his mind between music and a sense of wonder.

Although his father could not have known it, he was giving his son the perfect education for his eventual career. He introduced him not only to the blues of Muddy Waters and the gospel of Mahalia, but also to the jazz of Charlie Parker, the folk of Woody Guthrie and the country of Hank Williams and Jimmie Rodgers.

In 1950 George Ivan was enrolled at Elm Grove Primary School on the Beersbridge Road, and in 1956 – by now known as Van – he went on to Orangefield School for Boys, a progressive comprehensive school that was notable for employing both Catholics and Protestants on its staff.

Although he participated in the normal boyhood activities of the time – swimming in the nearby Beechie River, digging holes in the garden and roaming over building sites – it was noticed from

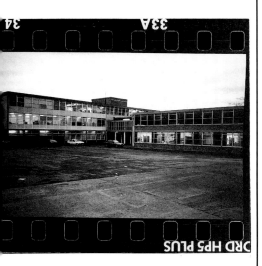

His parents, George and Violet Morrison (*above*, with Van), were a huge influence and encouragement in his musical career. Life at Orangefield School for Boys (*below*) failed to capture his imagination. "He slipped through school without making much impression," says one of his former schoolmasters.

Known as the Queen of Gospel Music, Mahalia Jackson (*above & right*) provided the young Van with what he would later regard as his first experience of spiritual ecstasy when he heard her voice on record. She died in 1972.

quite early on that he would rather observe than participate. He gained a reputation for being a "loner" or an "odd wee boy" who often seemed to be on the outside of events. One of his former teachers described him as always wearing "a furtive look . . . rather like a field hare".

"He wouldn't look at you he was so shy," says Nancy McCarter, a neighbour from Hyndford Street. "I can remember when he was a little boy I was standing outside my house because I'd locked myself out. A man I was talking to saw Van and asked him if he'd climb over my garden wall and go through the back door to let me in. He just shook his head and walked away."

Ethel Blakely, who lived next door to the Morrisons, has a similar memory: "If Van had come home from school and found me out the back speaking to his mum, he would have just walked past with his head down," she says. "He wouldn't have looked at his mum and he wouldn't have spoken to me. You could tell by his face that it was an effort for him even to come in."

When he was eleven years old he again witnessed the transports of delight that he had enjoyed while listening to Mahalia Jackson, but this time his experiences were unrelated to music and apparently unprovoked. Walking down the street he would suddenly be struck by a sense of timelessness, in which everything seemed beautiful and "right". This feeling could last for minutes or hours, or sometimes even for days.

It wasn't until years later that he was to read the works of poets and mystics who appeared to have had similar encounters. Colin Wilson, whose book *Poetry and Mysticism* was to influence him, described them as "intensity experiences". As a child, however, Van had kept quiet about them: "I didn't think there was even the possibility of talking to anyone about these feelings, and I didn't really feel the need," he says. "I'd feel similar things when I went to church, but even then I didn't feel like talking about it." When he did open up it was as an adult in songs like "Cyprus Avenue" and "Madame George", in which he hinted at powerful emotions that had overwhelmed him on a tree-lined street, near his home in East Belfast.

Van's father had an eclectic record collection which included work by blues artist Muddy Waters (*opposite, top left*), folk singer Woody Guthrie (*top right*), country musicians Hank Williams (*bottom left*, with wife Audrey) and Jimmie Rodgers (*bottom right*), and jazz saxophonist Charlie Parker (*above*). "I just grabbed as many Leadbelly and Guthrie and Hank Williams records as I could," said Van, "and tried to learn something."

The Morrisons were a fairly secular household, Protestant only inasmuch as they were not Roman Catholic. Van would go to Sunday school at the Brethren Gospel Hall in the street, or to the slightly more middle-class St Donard's, which was Church of Ireland. Then suddenly his mother became a Jehovah's Witness.

No one seems sure exactly how her conversion began or how long it lasted, but what is certain is that she became an ardent member of the local Kingdom Hall sometime during the 1950s. Some of the older members can still remember Van attending morning services with her, but George Morrison never made an appearance.

Her sudden conversion must have had an effect on her son, because if she was sincere in her beliefs she would have read the Bible to him regularly, and issued stern warnings about the dangers of leading a life outside the Lord. It also compounded his feeling of being an outsider: who else in Belfast had a father who played Jelly Roll Morton records, and a mother who indulged in doorstep evangelism?

"I was just on the periphery," he says of his contact with the local Kingdom Hall. "My mother went for a few years. We didn't go to church all the time, but it was a very churchy atmosphere in the sense that that's the way it is in Northern Ireland."

No one who knew Van during his school-days recalls his showing any interest in religion. Gil Irvine, a contemporary from Hyndford Street, is one of the few who can remember him being interested in study of any kind. "He was very good at soccer but he had no interest in it," says Irvine. "That seemed a bit strange to us at the time because all the other boys were really into sport. So, on the days when we were playing football or cricket, Van would go off and read. You would always find Van in the house with a book."

In 1956, when Van was ten years old, Lonnie Donegan prompted the British "skiffle" craze with his top ten hit "Rock Island Line". The appeal of skiffle was that it was simple and inexpensive to play. All that was needed was a Spanish guitar, a snare drum, a stand-up bass made from a broom handle attached to an empty tea-chest, and two chords.

Van's father visited America in the early 1950s and came back with presents of toys including a cowboy outfit and cowboy guns for his son (*above*). "I think he went to Detroit or Seattle," remembers Van's childhood friend Gil Irvine. "He brought me back a leather holster and that was a prized possession for many many years."

Van heard the records of pianist-composer Jelly Roll Morton (1885–1941) as a child and was impressed with this artist who combined elements of jazz, ragtime, blues, brass band and folk. He also became a fan of the folk-blues singer Huddie Leadbetter (*above right*), better known as Leadbelly, and was pleasantly surprised in 1956 to find Leadbelly's music kicking off the British skiffle craze when sung by Lonnie Donegan (*right*). "The major influence was Leadbelly," he once said: "If it wasn't for him I might never have been here."

Skiffle held an additional appeal for Van, because suddenly Donegan was popularising the strange music that his father had been listening to for years. "Rock Island Line" had been written by Huddie Ledbetter, better known as Leadbelly, who had become one of Van's favourite blues singers. "What I connected with was that I had been hearing Leadbelly before that, so when Donegan came along I thought everybody knew about it," Van has said. "Consequently I think I was really lucky to grow up at that time and hear what I heard then."

That year his father took him into the city centre to buy his first acoustic guitar. They called on Solly Lipsitz, the owner of Atlantic Records, a shop at 69 High Street that specialised in American jazz imports. "Van's father had brought him in quite a few times after I opened the shop in 1953," says Lipsitz. "This day, when he was looking for a guitar for Van, he asked me to come along with him and help to choose one. We went to a second-hand place called Smithfield Market and picked up something cheap."

Once he had the guitar, Van became wedded to his music. He learned basic chords from a songbook edited by folklorist Alan Lomax titled *The Carter Family Style*.

The following year he formed his first group with friends from around Hyndford Street. Next-door neighbour Walter Blakely played washboard, Billy Ruth played guitar, John McLean played tea-chest bass, and Gil Irvine played a home-made wind instrument they christened the "zobo". They called themselves the Sputniks after the newly launched Russian satellite, and began to play at Women's Institute meetings, school concerts and youth clubs. Like most skifflers they culled their material from what they heard being played by the new stars of skiffle, such as Donegan and Chas McDevitt.

The peak of the group's short career came in 1958, when they managed to book a spot during the children's matinées at a couple of local cinemas, the Willowfield on Woodstock Road, and the Strand on Holywood Road. "They showed films for kids on a Saturday morning and during the intervals they had a place for local entertainment," recalls Walter Blakely. "The audience was aged between seven and eleven. That was a big show for us."

The Sputniks drifted apart later that year, leaving Van free to play with some other local boys who were attending Belfast College of Technology.

George Jones, Billy McAllen and Roy Kane had started as a skiffle group that randomly picked its name from a pack of cards. One week they would play as the Jokers, the next as the Aces, then as the Jacks and so on. One of their regular appearances was on the back of a truck parked outside George Jones's house in Greenville Street. They would draw a crowd and then charge everyone threepence for the privilege of listening.

"One day this wee guy comes round and wants to join us," remembers Roy Kane. "This was Van. We told him we didn't need another guitar player because we already had two. That didn't deter him. He kept coming back and we kept telling him to clear off. Then someone had the brainwave of telling him to learn a different instrument and then come back to see us. He returned about three weeks later and had learned to play the saxophone."

Van had been struck on the saxophone since the previous year, when he had heard the Jimmy Giuffre 3s recording "The Train and the River", which featured Giuffre playing solos on both baritone and tenor sax. Van looked up a local teacher, George Cassidy, who taught him the rudiments of tenor sax and how to read music. Much to the consternation of his neighbours he began to practise in his room late at night. "I remember it vividly," says Walter Blakely, whose bedroom was separated from Van's by a thin brick wall. "Many's the time I shouted at him out of the window."

The three boys were impressed by Van's dedication and accepted him as a member of the group. George Jones and Billy McAllen were at that time playing Spanish guitars and Roy Kane, who was also the lead vocalist, had a plastic Eric Delaney snare drum with a cymbal hanging from it.

While still using names from playing cards they played venues like the East Belfast Working Men's Club (known locally as "the Hut"), the Brookborough Hall in Sandown Road and the Harriers Hall in Hyndford Street, carting their equipment with them on double-decker buses.

THE JIMMY GIUFFRE 3

CONTAINS BONUS TRACKS

"I was more into listening to a guy called Jimmy Giuffre than I was to rock'n'roll," Van has said. "I decided I wanted a sax when I heard Giuffre doing 'The Train and the River'. I couldn't get enough of it after that. If ever there's anyone who was a footnote or an asterisk it was him. He's my main influence on saxophone."

Jelly Roll Morton, pictured with his band in 1924, was the subject of the biography *Mr Jelly Roll* written by folklorist Alan Lomax. Van was to mention this book in "Cleaning Windows", his song of youthful reminiscence. "That's how I got into the business," he recounted in 1970. "That's how I got here – with Leadbelly and Woody Guthrie and Jelly Roll Morton and Ray Charles. That's what made me start singing."

In these semi-professional days groups were only loosely held together, which explains some of the problems in working out Van's CV around 1959 and 1960. Bill Dunn, a guitarist friend of George Jones's from Greenville Street, remembers working with Van in "at least four different bands" around this time, and the fabled Deanie Sands and the Javelins, often cited in books and articles as his first group, was simply another variation of the old line-up.

"The Javelins was me, George Jones, Van and Roy Kane," says Billy McAllen. "Deanie Sands was a girl called Evelyn Boucher who had had polio when she was a child and had callipers on her legs. She had a great voice and we used to mess about rehearsing after school."

In 1960 the four boys, along with keyboard player Wesley Black, became the Monarchs, and played cover versions of pop hits. In July of that year Van left Orangefield with no qualifications and no idea of a career beyond music.

"He slipped through school without making much impression," recalls his former English master, David Hammond. "I say that out of admiration rather than as a criticism. If he'd listened to people like me he would never have written a line. He believed in nobody but himself."

His parents worried about him. In their working-class community in which most men worked for either the shipbuilders Harland & Wolff or the aerospace manufacturers Short Brothers, it was expected that boys would apprentice themselves to a trade. But Van showed no interest in following in his father's footsteps.

Despite Van's protestations his mother went ahead and persuaded a neighbour, George McDowell, to accept her son as an apprentice at the engineering firm Musgrave & Co., where he was a foreman.

"He started as an apprentice fitter," remembers Tommy Hanna, who worked briefly at Musgrave's alongside Van. "But it wasn't a job that he took to. You could see that his heart was elsewhere. He didn't want to be there and the foreman didn't really want him to be there either."

His involvement in the world of structural steel engineering lasted only a few weeks. "He'd come to us against his will," says McDowell. "He was only there because his mother wanted him to be. He never developed any relationship with the boys in the shop because he was like a conscript. He was there on sufferance.

"His heart was in his music but you would never have thought that he would have made the grade as a performer if you'd spoken to him. You could hardly get a word out of him. But engineering definitely wasn't his scene. That's why he left."

After a brief period in a meat-cleaning factory, Van teamed up with a friend and began cleaning windows in the streets around Hyndford Street.

THE MONARCHS SHOWBAND

The Monarchs showband circa 1961, photographed for a publicity hand-out at the King George VI Hall in Belfast. Back row, left to right: Ronnie (trombone), Davey Bell (sax), Jimmy Law (vocals), Roy Kane (drums) and Wesley Black (keyboards). Front row, left to right: Billy McAllen (guitar), Van Morrison (sax), Leslie Holmes (trumpet) and George Jones (bass).

CHAPTER TWO

CLEANING WINDOWS

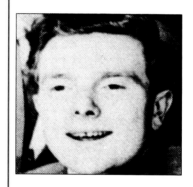

The Monarchs circa 1963. Clockwise from bottom left: Van Morrison (tenor sax), George Jones (bass), Billy McAllen (guitar), Harry Megahey (baritone sax and trumpet), Wesley Black (keyboards), Lawrie McQueen (drums) and George Hethrington (vocals). McQueen and Hethrington joined the band in Scotland and left while in Germany.

IN HIS SONG "Cleaning Windows" Van sketched the details of his life during 1961 and 1962, and captured the balance between his contentment at work and his aspirations to learn more about music. It conveyed the impression that his happiness with the mundane routine of smoking Woodbine cigarettes, eating Paris buns and drinking lemonade was made possible by the promise that at the end of the day he could enter the world of books and records: a Jack Kerouac paperback on his lap and Muddy Waters on the gramophone.

Like many creative writers, he was happy with his own company. The introversion that had marked him out as a shy and lonely boy was not, for Van, an inadequacy but a diversion of energy. He preferred thinking to doing, observing to participating.

In the song Van refers to "Sam", his partner Sammy Woodburn. "He was a Ted with a big drape coat," remembers Roy Kane. "He had naturally curly hair and a wild turn in his eye. The two of them used to clean windows around the terraced houses in the area. Wee Van always used to do the downstairs windows because he couldn't climb up the ladders."

The beauty of the job was that it allowed a great degree of independence. There was no pressure to socialise, no need to wear a uniform, and it allowed Van the opportunity to take time off to rehearse or play.

The saxophone "blowing" referred to in the song had now been incorporated into his performance with the Monarchs, which had developed into a conventional Irish showband, through the addition of a singer and two brass players from south west Belfast.

As Van explained to *Now Dig This* magazine in December 1991: "We became a showband because in Ireland you had to have more bodies to work. Groups weren't really happening. They were happening everywhere else with the Shadows etc. etc. but for some reason the [Irish] promoters didn't want groups.

"They hated 'guitars, bass and drums' groups. They just didn't want to know. You had to have a horn section. You couldn't work properly if you didn't. All the showbands had horn sections and a lot of them were really good, like the Royal Showband, the Dixielanders, the Swingtime Aces, Clipper Carlton . . . The horn sections were the main thing. So you had to have at least a seven- or eight-piece band to work."

Roy Kane remembers the change taking place fairly suddenly. "I forget exactly how it came about but all of a sudden we were a seven- or eight-piece showband. I remember going to Jackson's the tailors where we got jackets made. Jimmy Law, the singer, was in yellow and all the rest of us were in shocking pink."

Although Van was not the main vocalist at this point, he was beginning to build a reputation as a flamboyant performer who would roll around on stage, dance on tables and climb on the singer's shoulders while playing the sax.

Herbie Armstrong, a local guitarist who played in a band called the Twilights, remembers seeing the Monarchs at Carrickfergus Town Hall in 1961. "Van was amazing," he recalls. "He was sitting on the singer's shoulders playing the saxophone. He was a tremendous showman. He wasn't supposed to be the focus of the group but he's the one I really remembered."

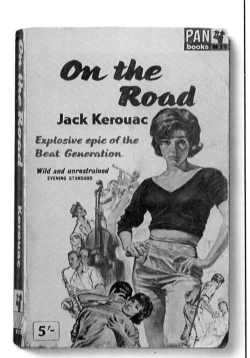

Jack Kerouac's "beat generation" novels *On the Road* and *Dharma Bums* portrayed a search for spiritual enlightenment through drugs, music and Eastern meditation. Van first read them as a teenager living on Hyndford Street.

'Crazy-mixed-up novel about frustrated youth getting nowhere fast'

Manchester Evening News

Friends were surprised at the transformation that came over him once he got on stage. Tommy Hanna, who had worked with him at Musgrave's, can remember going with him to a dance hall in Dundonald to see Johnny Johnston and the Midnighters, a local group with a hot reputation. At this point Hanna had no idea that Van could sing, and was taken aback when he was told that he was going to be doing a guest spot following the intermission.

"I can't remember all the numbers he did," Hanna says, "but I can specifically remember him doing 'I Go Ape' [a hit for Neil Sedaka in 1959]. When he started singing I was absolutely astounded. He was wearing a smart Burton's suit with a white shirt, and he took his jacket off and threw it among the girls. He then jumped off stage and rolled around on the floor. When he got back up his shirt was as black as your boot.

"Whenever Johnston came back to start his set up again they wouldn't let Van off. They wanted him to do the rest of the gig. It was amazing because he was such a quiet fellow and yet when he heard the music he came alive."

Band member Roy Kane concurs with this view: "Van was a complete nutter on stage. We had one number based on a blues riff called 'Daddy Cool', and during this he used to throw himself on the floor, split his trousers and throw his shirt off."

In 1962 the Monarchs were offered work in Scotland, which meant giving up their day jobs and turning professional. Roy Kane, who was working in the furniture department of his local Co-op, was the only member who decided to remain in Belfast. The rest of the group left for Glasgow, where they found a replacement drummer, Lawrie McQueen, and a new vocalist, George Hethrington. They moved in with their new manager, Frank Cunningham, who lived in a council house in Pollock, and rehearsed in his garden.

Over the next few months they toured extensively around Scotland, and began to move in the direction of rhythm and blues, under the influence of Hethrington, who was a big fan of Ray Charles. Then, despite their lack of accommodation or guaranteed work, they decided to move down to London.

Ray Charles became an influence on the Monarchs through the enthusiasm of vocalist George Hethrington. He remains one of Van's musical heroes to this day.

In the early 1960s the Shadows were the archetypal British beat group. Their sartorial code set the standard and was even to affect the early Beatles.

On their arrival they were forced to live rough, sleeping either in or under their van at night, washing at the public toilets in Leicester Square, and taking their meals in cheap cafés around Soho. However, fortune smiled on them when they encountered Don Charles, a singer they had worked with in Scotland, who was now a minor star after having a top forty hit with "Walk with Me My Angel" early in 1962.

Charles allowed them to use his flat to get cleaned up, and then introduced them to his booking agent, Ruby Bard, who also looked after the trad jazz band the Temperance Seven, and singer Georgie Fame, who at that time had a residency at the Flamingo Club. Bard obtained work for the Monarchs in the London area, particularly in Irish clubs, and then managed to book a tour of clubs in Germany, where they would play in Heidelberg, Frankfurt and Cologne.

Right: A Glasgow newspaper reports the strange arrival of the "International Monarchs". Van is pictured third from the left. The group's sole recording session took place at Ariola Studios, Cologne. *Opposite, top:* Roy Kane on vocals with Van Morrison and Harry Megahey on saxophones. *Opposite, bottom:* The same trio plus George Jones on vocals and Wesley Black at the keyboards. Black was tragically gunned down by terrorists in February 1975.

Pollok's garden jam session

HOUSEWIVES and children in the Levernside Road district of Pollok have had a foot-tapping time this week—to the live music of the International Monarchs band.

Several of the septet — who come from Belfast and Glasgow — have been staying with their manager, Mr. Frank Cunningham at No. 33 before starting a tour of Scotland on Thursday. And his large corner garden and the sunny weather made the open air a natural rehearsal spot.

As the boys played — hooked up with amplifiers and microphone — shoppers and schoolchildren joined the free treat.

Vocalist is Gerry Hotherington, aged ...

of Mount Florida, who went to Belfast a few weeks ago to fix up dates for his own part time band during their holidays. He was introduced to the Monarchs — George James, Van Morrison, Billy McAllan, Harry Mac, and Blackie — and the result was he signed on professionally with the band.

He later got his own drummer, Lawrie McQueen, of 74 Kempsthorn Road, Pollok, into the group, which has just finished a tour of Ireland.

After touring Scotland, the boys move to England and sometime in August they hope to tour Germany.

At the time Germany was regarded as an ideal training ground for young groups, who would be worked long and hard in order to cater for the tastes of an audience who had an apparently insatiable appetite for the latest British and American dance hits. The Monarchs were expected to play from eight in the evening until three in the morning seven nights a week, with afternoon matinées on Saturdays and Sundays.

"Van started to go down really well with the American servicemen who used to come to the clubs, so the owner rang Ruby Bard and asked if he could book us for another month," recalls Billy McAllen. "So we did a second month in Heidelberg, and then moved on to the Storeyville Club in Frankfurt."

But during this period in Frankfurt problems arose with the two Scottish members, who were drinking so hard that they had to be sacked. The vocals were not a problem to cover, because each band member took it in turn to sing, but drummer Lawrie McQueen also had to be replaced, and so they recontacted Roy Kane. "I had this call at work one day telling me how great the German scene was," says Kane. "It coincided with my having a row with my boss, so I got a ticket and flew out."

Above: **The Monarchs posing for a publicity photo, with Van on the extreme right.** *Left:* **Recording in Cologne.** *Top:* **Harry Megahey, Van Morrison, Wesley Black, George Jones, Oliver Trimble (substitute vocalist flown over on George Hethrington's departure), Billy McAllen and Roy Kane.** *Bottom:* **Billy McAllen, Van Morrison, Oliver Trimble, Wesley Black, George Jones, producer Ron Kovaks and Harry Megahey.**

The group was encouraged in its rhythm and blues direction by an audience largely composed of black American servicemen. "It was the GIs who got us into it," says McAllen. "They would take us up to their camps and let us hear the latest records from America. Van was already deeply into this music, and I think he enjoyed playing to an American audience for the first time in his life."

The Storeyville Club in Cologne was a different scene. Here they found themselves confronted with wild German teenagers who were obsessed with the Beatles – who had recently undergone their own apprenticeship in Hamburg – and wanted to hear nothing but cover versions of Merseybeat hits.

Ron Kovacs of CBS Records in Germany saw them at the Storeyville one night, and offered them a flat fee to record two trashy pop songs, "Boozoo Hully Gully" and "Twingy Baby". Although none of the group liked the songs they welcomed the experience of recording, and so they went in to Ariola Studios and cut the two songs.

The Monarchs in concert, with Van third from the left.

After returning from Cologne in November 1963, the Monarchs broke up. And just a few weeks later, they learned that "Boozoo Hully Gully" had become a hit single in Germany.

But by this time Van and Billy McAllen had joined their mate Geordie Sproule in the Manhattan Showband. Van then persuaded Herbie Armstrong, whose band the Twilights had just disintegrated, to join them on guitar. They played weekend dates in England, performing mainly at Irish clubs. During this time Van became aware of the burgeoning rhythm and blues scene that had thrown up groups like the Yardbirds and the Rolling Stones. In Newcastle they saw the Alan Price Set (as the Animals were then known), and in London they heard of the Pretty Things and John Mayall's Bluesbreakers.

Back in Belfast Van had always been considered a little weird, because of his obsession with musicians like Muddy Waters and John Lee Hooker. But now these same musicians had become the inspiration for a new generation of rock stars.

In March 1964 the Manhattan Showband played at a Saint Patrick's night show at an Irish ballroom in Camden Town, London, and afterwards were allowed to stay on in a spare bedroom over the venue.

The previous night Van and Herbie Armstrong had visited Ken Colyer's Club at Studio '51 in Soho, to hear the rhythm and blues session. The headlining act was the Downliners Sect, a blues band with what was then considered exceptionally long hair, who played a mixture of Jimmy Reed and Bo Diddley numbers.

"I think Van had had the idea of forming an R & B group before that night, but when he saw the Downliners Sect he said, that's it, that's the sort of group I want to have," says Herbie Armstrong. "I remember him asking if he could blow harmonica with them but they said it was too late. He wasn't known to anyone then."

Back in Camden Armstrong remembers Van playing him a song he had recently written. "We were both drinking cider and leaping up and down on these army-style beds, when he told me he'd written a song," he recalls. "It was called 'Could

STUDIO '51
10/11 GT. NEWPORT ST.
LEICESTER SQUARE
RHYTHM & BLUES every
Friday, 8 to Midnight
THE DOWNLINERS SECT
Saturday Afternoon, 4 until 6.30
THE DOWNLINERS SECT
Monday, 8-11
THE DOWNLINERS SECT
Thursday, 8-11
THE MULESKINNERS
Non-members admitted at all Sessions
Apply NOW for membership, 5/- to
March '65
Next R&B Session March 21/28

"The first British R&B I heard was the Downliners Sect," said Van. "It was at the Ken Colyer Club [Studio '51]. They were really doing it then. I heard the Pretty Things later. But the Downliners Sect were it." The group, which never had a hit, began recording in 1964 and disbanded in 1967. It consisted of (left to right) Ray Stone (drums), Terry Gibson (guitar), Don Crane (vocals), Johnny Sutton (guitar, autoharp) and Keith Grant (bass).

You Would You'. I thought it was incredible. I had never known anyone who had written a song before."

On his arrival back in Belfast, there was a message waiting for Armstrong inviting him to join the Golden Eagles, the Plaza Ballroom's resident eleven-piece showband led by Brian Rossi.

A lunchtime disc jockey and eccentric rock'n'roll entertainer, Rossi was a hero to Belfast's up-and-coming musicians. He had toured Britain, appeared on bills with idols like Billy Fury and Gene Vincent, and was handicapped only by his age (30 in 1964) and a receding hairline. In 1991 Van remembered Rossi as the "first person I saw who was rock'n'roll" when he came across him in the late fifties, playing piano with a back-up trio of two guitars and drums. "He was the happening thing in Belfast," recalled Van.

"To be asked to join Rossi's group was the dream of every musician in the city at the time," says Armstrong. "You had made it if you played with him. Rossi was a hero to both Van and myself.

"After I got this invitation I went to a phone box at the end of the street and phoned him up, and he asked me to audition the next day.

Of Belfast rock'n'roll hero Brian Rossi, Van has said: "He was the first person that I saw who was 'rock'n'roll'. He was playing at the Plaza Ballroom . . . and he was the happening thing in Belfast."

Band leader Brian Rossi at the Plaza Ballroom.

A FEATHER IN THE CAPS OF THE GOLDEN EAGLES

Locally-formed band to be resident at Plaza

WITH the tap of glittering, white-shod feet, the Belfast Plaza Ballroom's first locally-formed resident showband will swing into rip-roaring action for the first time to-night.

And the drums of big Brian Rossi with his Golden Eagles will beat out a revolution in Mecca dancing. For this is the first time in the Belfast ballroom's 22-year-life that an almost all-Ulster band takes the stage as a resident, five-night-a-week feature.

Mecca policy formerly dictated that cross-Channel bands supply the music—the Plaza is, of course, owned by Mecca Dancing — but new Ulster-born manager, Bob Herron, has negotiated a policy switch to give a local group a chance.

Nine men — including one Scot—and two teenage Belfast girls make up the Golden Eagles. Uniforms are white with a shimmer of gold thread

sewn in. Except for the Scot, all the group are Ulster-born and have worked with local showbands in Northern Ireland.

Disc-jockey

Belfast - born rock singer, Brian Rossi, is no stranger to the Plaza. For the leader of the new group is a lunch-time disc-jockey at the ballroom's after-noon dancing sessions.

Rossi has made extensive singing tours of England and Scotland, appearing with such pop kings as Gene Vincent, Billy Fury and The Shadows.

In two grinding weeks, Rossi managed to comb through the local music world and put his group together for to-night's debut. Rehearsals have been tough and crammed.

The Golden Eagles have a new £500 Hammond organ among their equipment, and for pop fans they promise jazz, twist, rock-and-roll and, of course—the madison.

"Van was in the box with me and he nudged me and said, ask him if they're looking for a saxophone player. Rossi said they weren't but they were looking for a singer. I put my hand over the mouthpiece and said, they're looking for a singer. Van said, tell him I can sing."

The next day the two rehearsed Chuck Berry songs at Armstrong's home in Glenmachan Road, and were then taken to the audition in a butcher's van, to avoid being seen by anyone connected with the Manhattan Showband.

"We carried on rehearsing amongst the carcasses in the back of the van, and then when we got there we found it was all these men who looked really ancient," remembers Armstrong. "They were probably in their early thirties, but they had Aran sweaters and were smoking pipes. They were used to playing dance music and top ten hits, but Van wanted them to play 'Hoochie Coochie Man' and then 'Bye Bye Johnny'.

"After he'd finished we were both told that we could start that night. We did exactly that and they really loved him. It was a huge dance orchestra and Van blew everyone's minds."

Van's memories of the period consist of his playing harmonica and tenor sax, and being given a special spot to sing Ray Charles numbers like "Sticks and Stones" and "What'd I Say". It wasn't exactly a beat group explosion, but it earned him a regular eleven pounds a week.

"Then, during this period, there was an advert in the *Belfast Evening Telegraph* that blew me away when I read it," recalls Van. "It said, 'Musicians wanted to start R & B club.' I went and met these guys . . . and they said that they wanted to start this R & B club, and they were looking for people [to play]. There was only me and this other guy who showed up."

The advert had been placed by three music fans, named Jerry, Jerry and Jimmy, who became known to everyone as "the three Js".

According to Van he found a room at the Maritime Hotel, a mission run for seamen, and then "had to just get musicians in at short notice as the people I really wanted I couldn't get. I got another lot of people and we went into this club as Them."

Brian Rossi *and the* Golden Eagles

When Van joined Brian Rossi's Golden Eagles it was one of the most secure jobs for a Belfast musician, but he left to join the little-known Gamblers which was shortly to become known as Them. Brian Rossi moved to Blackpool in England where he died of bronchial pneumonia in 1984.

The musicians he "wanted but couldn't get" must have been bass player Tito Tinsley and guitarist Herbie Armstrong, both of whom were reluctant to leave their new-found security with the Golden Eagles. And the other "lot of people" was clearly the Gamblers, a four-piece outfit formed in 1962 by Billy Harrison (guitar) and Alan Henderson (bass), who were veering towards the Bo Diddley and Chuck Berry end of rock'n'roll, and finding it difficult to obtain gigs in Belfast, where pop songs and Shadows uniformity were the order of the day.

Whether Van "got" the Gamblers or the Gamblers offered Van a job remains unclear. Possibly both stories are true: Van's search for a band with potential coincided with the Gamblers' attempt to expand their line-up.

The group's keyboard player, Eric Wrixon, was a cousin of Billy McAllen's, and had heard that Van was dissatisfied with showband life. "I decided that we needed another person in the group," says Wrixon. "I also knew that Van was interested in doing something different."

"No one would really listen to what we were doing at the time," recalls Alan Henderson. "None of the dance halls wanted to know, because the Liverpool sound was what was going on, not rhythm and blues.

"We were into the rhythm and blues scene with the Gamblers, but we didn't have the information that we needed. That came when we met up with Van, because he had such a fantastic knowledge of the music which he'd learned from hearing the records his father played."

The Gamblers, like Van, were tired of the smart-suit look that characterised Irish bands of the time. Van had once suggested to Bill Dunn that they formed a group in which the musicians wore long johns and old vests, rather than mohair suits and ties. This was the first indication of his desire to play the game on his own terms.

"I think he liked the fact that we were unconventional," says Billy Harrison. "We weren't doing what everyone else was doing. We had been through a period when we all dressed alike, but we got fed up with it. We were four individuals and we wore what we fancied wearing."

They started rehearsing together, and playing songs like Bobby Bland's "Turn on Your Love Light". Then Eric Wrixon came up with a name for the new band. "I think it was a reaction to the fact that everyone was called the 'somethings' – the Fendertones, the Stratotones. I think it was the first time anyone had given themselves a name that was a single word. We were going to be known simply as Them."

CHAPTER THREE

THE STORY OF THEM

The shortest-lived version of Them (*left*) featured Joe Boni (lead guitar), Terry Noone (drums), Peter Bardens (keyboards), Van Morrison (vocals) and Alan Henderson (bass).

ON FRIDAY 17TH APRIL 1964 Them made their first appearance at the Maritime Hotel. During the immediate run-up, the three Js placed teaser adverts on the entertainment page of the *Belfast Telegraph*. On Tuesday they asked "Who are? What are? THEM", on Wednesday, "When? And where? Will you see THEM", on Thursday, "Rhythm and Blues and THEM. When?" and finally they announced that Them, "Ireland's Specialists in Rhythm and Blues", would be playing at the Maritime Hotel that evening at 8:30.

The Maritime Hotel was an unlikely location from which to start a musical movement. It was a plain, ugly building (built as a police station at the turn of the century and now demolished), that provided accommodation and entertainment for sailors. Because the management had religious affiliations the hotel was not licensed to sell alcohol, but it had a 200-capacity ballroom that it had been renting out to local promoters since 1959.

A week of teaser adverts on the entertainments page of the *Belfast Telegraph* created an air of expectancy for the début performance of "Ireland's Specialists in Rhythm and Blues".

The group rehearsed at Billy Harrison's home, and in a rented attic room above Dougie Knight's bicycle shop in Great Victoria Street, in the city centre. Knight was an important figure to Belfast blues aficionados. He had been importing American albums since the early 1950s, and selling them alongside the cycle accessories. Later he had organised evening record-listening sessions, which Van would attend, and in 1960 he had brought Memphis Slim, Jesse Fuller, Little Brother Montgomery and Champion Jack Dupree to Belfast.

"There were very few people there on the first night," remembers Billy Harrison. "There were a hell of a lot the next week, and on the third week they were queuing to get in from six o'clock onwards.

"The thing just took off on that third week, and the Maritime Hotel became a place that people made pilgrimages to. It became the fount of blues learning for Ireland."

Van has recollected that Them "lived and died as a group on the stage at the Maritime Hotel in Belfast", and claimed that nothing on tape ever came close to capturing the feel of those appearances of the spring and summer of 1964. "We ran the place," he has said. "Even when it came to making records we were out of our element

Dougie Knight, pictured here in 1956, ran a bicycle shop in Belfast which also sold imported American blues records. Van was a regular customer and Them's earliest rehearsals took place in an attic above the shop.

The Maritime Hotel, where Them made its début on 17th April 1964, was a police station converted into a mission for seamen; it was hosting a rhythm and blues club on Friday nights designed to appeal to local university and art college students. Even though they only played there for a short season, Van has since said that Them "lived and died as a group on the stage at the Maritime Hotel".

. . . The way we did the numbers at the Maritime was more spontaneous, more energetic, more everything, because we were feeding off the crowd."

Peter Lloyd, an electronics student at Queen's University, was the first to record the group. After eliciting a song from them for a rag week promotion, he coaxed them back to tape "Turn on Your Love Light", which was generally regarded as the most popular number from their Maritime shows. The result was then taken to Mervyn Solomon, a 34-year-old record distributor who worked for his father's company, Solomon and Peres, and had trained with Decca Records in New York before opening a recording studio in Belfast in 1953.

The original line-up of Them was (left to right) Alan Henderson, Van Morrison, Eric Wrixon (keyboards), Ronnie Millings (drums) and Billy Harrison.

Solomon was interested in what he heard. He checked them out at the Maritime, and although he had doubts about the musicianship, he was impressed by Van both as a singer and as a performer, and could see that the group were arousing excitement among the student-age audience. "They were probably the most different group around," says Solomon. "Van had a lot of jazz in his voice, and I had been a jazz musician most of my life, so I was very taken with that. Also, in those days he used to move around a lot. He used to do the splits on stage and run from side to side."

Solomon arranged for the group to come to his home, where they ran through their repertoire on acoustic guitars. Satisfied with what he heard, he alerted his brother, Phil Solomon, a successful show business manager in London. He in turn contacted Dick Rowe, the then head of a & r for Decca Records, who came to Belfast to hear the group for himself.

Rowe didn't rush to make a decision. His great triumph had been in signing the Rolling Stones to Decca, but he was better known for his great failure, not signing the Beatles. When he finally signed them the contract was made between Decca and Phil Solomon, and the five members of the group were in turn signed to Solomon. As Van was still only 18 his father had to sign on his behalf.

Within weeks of the signing, Them were taken to London to record their first tracks in Decca's studios in West Hampstead. At this point Eric Wrixon left the group because he was studying for A level exams, and his parents didn't want him to turn professional. His place was taken by Patrick John McAuley.

American publicity photo of the most recognisable version of Them at the time of "Baby Please Don't Go".

Right: Eric Wrixon left Them just prior to the group's leaving for England and was replaced by Patrick John McAuley (back row, far right). The Belfast events magazine *City Week* (*below*) monitored the changes in the group.

AT LAST—AN ALL BELFAST GROUP AGAIN

THEM

of the Ulster R&B
on the music of the
use at the group's

use backing-band
isburn hall have
on around them.
of the material
what they may
jazz that would
her local group,
t critics stayed
boy Ray Elliott
r version of the
rain and The
wband fan who

to the band, no
eir way back to
cination

The new THEM, John Wil...

The first recording session, on 5th July 1964, was produced by Rowe, who, having decided that McAuley and drummer Ronnie Millings were weak links in the chain, instructed musical director Arthur Greenslade to cover on organ and brought in Bobby Graham, a top session drummer.

"The boys got needled when they saw these session men, and so we had both organs playing and put the drummers in separate booths, but we only recorded one organ and one drum track," remembers Mervyn Solomon. "They just weren't proficient enough at that point." (Alan Henderson denies that Millings wasn't miked up, and claims that Them was the first rock group to record using two drummers.)

During that first session they recorded "Groovin", "You Can't Judge a Book by Its Cover", "Turn on Your Love Light", "Don't Start Crying Now", "One Two Brown Eyes", "Philosophy" and "Gloria".

Although not released as the A side of a Them single in Britain, "Gloria" was to become the classic

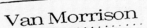

Van Morrison

THEM singer Van Morrison is undoubtedly the most successful individual musician to rise out of the Irish group scene—and that includes Ian Whitcomb. A string of British, American and Continental smash hits he has to his credit, some of them his own royalty-winning compositions. Versatile, too. He plays an assortment of instruments and has never been anything but a professional musician since he left school.

PERSONALITY FILE

NAME: Ivan Morrison.

BORN: Belfast, 31st August, 1945.

DESCRIPTION: Height: 5' 7"; blue eyes; fair hair now cut shortish.

CAREER HIGHLIGHTS: Born into musical family (father a jazz and blues disc collector, mother an accomplished musician). Toured Germany with the Monarchs in 1964. Joined the Gamblers (now THEM) in spring 64.

INSTRUMENTS PLAYED: Vocalist, harmonica, saxophone, guitar, various percussion.

RECORDS: About two dozen. Including hits 'Gloria', 'Baby, Please Don't Go', 'Here Comes the Night', 'Mystic Eyes', 1 EP, 1 album.

COMPOSITIONS: Include 'Gloria', 'Mystic Eyes', 'If You and I [. . . .] 'Little Girl', 'You Just Can't Win', 'I Like It Like That'. Currently four other groups have recorded his compositions. Literally scores of other songs and instrumentals.

FAVOURITE ARTISTES: Bobby Bland, Sam Cooke, Otis Redding, Booker T, Stevie Winwood, the Animals.

LIKES: Girls, walking in the country, swimming, keeping busy, fans, Paris, poetry.

AMBITION: To make it . . .

**Profile taken from *City Week*
magazine, 25th November 1965.**

Van Morrison track from this period, and would later provide inspiration for the American "garage band" phenomenon. It had a hypnotic riff, a solid drum beat and a vocal performance that went from the cooingly seductive to the snarlingly nasty.

The song resulted from the joint efforts of Van, Billy Harrison and Alan Henderson during one of their early rehearsals, and formed a part of their set by the time they reached the Maritime. Whether Van was the sole author has been a subject of debate. The agreement with Phil Solomon was that if Van had written the words, it was deemed to be a Morrison song.

"If I were a hard-nosed barrister I would argue that some of the royalties from that song should be shared with Billy Harrison," says Eric Wrixon. "It was Billy who came up with the riff, but I think Van was presented with a form to sign by the Solomons that assumed he was the sole songwriter in the group."

The true identity of Gloria has never been made clear. Wrixon recollects a woman named Gloria who was around during the Maritime days, and with whom Van would "disappear from time to time", but neighbours in Hyndford Street are convinced that the song is a disguised tribute to Van's cousin, Gloria Gordon, who died of cancer while the Monarchs were away in Germany. "She was quite an influence on Van," remembers Walter Blakely. "They were very close, almost like brother and sister. When she died she was only in her mid-twenties and had a little baby daughter. It was a terrible shock for him."

On 4th September 1964 the first single, "Don't Start Crying Now", was released in Britain. It didn't make the charts, and the group found themselves being booked into inappropriate venues.

"We died a death," admits Harrison. "We found ourselves booked into Irish clubs and working men's clubs, which were the wrong places to book a rhythm and blues group.

"There were gigs we went to where we just turned the wagon round and didn't even bother going in. We just said, bollocks, we're not playing here."

In October 1964 they recorded "Baby Please Don't Go", a number credited to Big Joe Williams, but later found to have been composed by Papa

When Them first arrived in England they suffered from having to play in unsuitable venues, but the above gig, scheduled for 15th October 1964, would have attracted London's R&B aficionados.

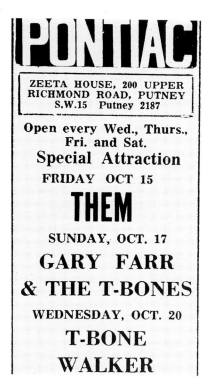

PONTIAC

ZEETA HOUSE, 200 UPPER RICHMOND ROAD, PUTNEY S.W.15 Putney 2187

Open every Wed., Thurs., Fri. and Sat.
Special Attraction
FRIDAY OCT 15

THEM

SUNDAY, OCT. 17

GARY FARR & THE T-BONES

WEDNESDAY, OCT. 20

T-BONE WALKER

Harvey Hull and Long Cleeve Reid in the 1920s. Van was introduced to the track by Dougie Knight.

"I suggested the idea of John Lee Hooker's version," says Knight. "I liked the way Hooker had done it because it was really in a sonata form, where the theme is stated then taken apart before being restated at the end, and that was the way Van's mind was working at the time.

"He was trying to create thematic material rather than songs with obvious beginnings, middles and ends. I had said that the lack of dynamic range was a flaw in pop music. You had to have music where something soft could be a climax as well as something loud, and where tension wasn't always related to volume."

Jimmy Page, at that time one of London's brightest young session guitarists, was brought in for the recording by Dick Rowe; he played a lick on it inspired by Paul Burlisson's riff on "Train Kept a-Rollin", by Johnny Burnette and the Rock'n'Roll Trio. He played some rhythm fills but would later be credited with creating the impressive lead riff, something which both Alan Henderson and Billy Harrison deny was the case.

On 6th November 1964 "Baby Please Don't Go" was released in England, and had "Gloria" as its flip-side. This coincided with another shuffle of group membership, as drummer Ronnie Millings returned to Belfast, because life on the road wasn't providing him with enough money to send home. Patrick John McAuley moved from keyboards to take his place, and for a short while they worked as a four-piece band, until McAuley's brother Jackie took over on keyboards.

In December 1964 the new line-up made its television début on *Ready Steady Go*, on a bill that featured the Rolling Stones. But the group's lack of finances forced them to use their fee to pay off their debts, before returning to Belfast for Christmas.

A fortnight later they learned that "Baby Please Don't Go" had entered the British charts, and that the song was going to be played each week over the opening credits of *Ready Steady Go*, at that time the most dynamic pop music show on British television.

In January 1965 they returned to London, where Phil Solomon introduced them to Bert Berns, a

Opposite: Them appeared on the British television show *Ready Steady Go* in December 1964 to play their new single "Baby Please Don't Go". Patrick John McAuley was temporarily moved to drums when Ronnie Millings left.

The group became closely identified with *Ready Steady Go* and its mod optimism when "Baby Please Don't Go" began being used over the show's credits. The song had been introduced to Van by Dougie Knight (*bottom*) who played him a version by John Lee Hooker.

The most familiar Them line-up came when Patrick John McAuley's brother Jackie (far left) joined the group on keyboards.

producer who he felt might be able to harness the raw potential of the group and turn it into something more chart-worthy. Berns was an American who'd co-written the hit single "Twist and Shout" (which had been covered by the Beatles), and whom Solomon had met the previous year at a Decca Records convention.

"I liked the feel of the stuff that Bert Berns was doing," says Mervyn Solomon. "He liked Van and he didn't think he was being taken down the right road with the material that we were doing. He thought we should have gone more pop."

The first track that Berns cut with Them, after lengthy rehearsals in Soho, was "Here Comes the Night", one of his own compositions. Again session musicians were used to bolster the sound. Phil Coulter, an old friend of the group from Belfast, played keyboards and Andy White drummed.

"The British sound of the time was very clinical," recalls Billy Harrison. "It was BBC-ish because the BBC had set recording standards for everyone. It had to be note- and word-perfect. Berns introduced an American sound to Them. He created an atmosphere in the studio. He really got something going."

"Here Comes the Night" justified the Solomons' faith in Bert Berns. It had enough rhythmic novelty to assure it airplay, and enough soul to ensure that Them were not accused of selling out.

Three weeks after its release it entered the British charts, and finally peaked at number 2. Two months after its British release it entered the American charts, where it reached a high of 24.

However, at the time when the group should have been capitalising on their international success, they fell victim to internal squabbles, and began a bad relationship with the press.

In interviews they appeared to be competing with each other, to see who could be the least co-operative. When Keith Altham of *New Musical Express* spoke to them, Billy Harrison cleaned his nails with a jack-knife, while Van Morrison sat in a corner with Bert Berns. Judith Simons of the *Daily Express* found it impossible to elicit a coherent sentence from the group. And *Melody Maker* reported that the group was "switched off to such

The group were successfully produced by American songwriter-producer Bert Berns (*top*) but later less successfully by British songwriter Tommy Scott (*bottom*) who was a friend of Phil and Mervyn Solomon.

During 1965 the group, which was perceived as being in the same R&B mould as the Rolling Stones, toured extensively and gained in confidence. The keyboardless group (*opposite*) lasted only a few weeks.

an extent that it is excessively difficult to cull enough words from them to form a sentence".

Van's impatience with categorisations was evident even in these early days. "We don't call ourselves an R & B group or anything," he said. "We just let the public decide what they want to call the music we play."

Phil Solomon, who had been used to organising uncontroversial acts like Ruby Murray and the Bachelors, was exasperated by their behaviour. "They were impossible," he says today. "Some of them were taking drugs. They were completely uncontrollable."

And Mervyn Solomon remembers one particular day, when his brother had arranged a midday press conference for the group at their offices in Great Marlborough Street, and the group arrived an hour late and as high as kites. "I remember that Philip booted Van down the stairs that day," he says. "From that day on it was very much a manager and his act. He didn't like him after that. Van could be a very strange boy, very moody."

Irresponsible behaviour coupled with a refusal to communicate was a publicity nightmare, until the Solomons hit on the idea of transforming the moodiness into a selling point. The sullen looks and the reluctant mumbles could be made to work for the group if they could be projected as a deliberate attitude, an inarticulate frustration with the world.

Decca Records had enjoyed great success with the Rolling Stones, another group who rarely smiled or joined in the normal hand-shaking, teeth-baring publicity routine, and so they invented what they proudly called the Angry Young Them (a play on the "Angry Young Men" label attached to a group of young British writers in the 1950s that included playwright John Osborne and novelist Kingsley Amis).

Just as Them were about to start recording their début album in May 1965, "internal strife" resulted in Jackie McAuley leaving the group, and Peter Bardens from the Cheynes (whose drummer was Mick Fleetwood) joining on keyboards.

Berns returned to America after producing one Morrison song, "Little Girl"; his role was then taken over by Tommy Scott, a friend of the Solomons who was better known as a minor

The fifth incarnation of Them
saw Jackie McAuley (*left*, at top
of picture) replaced on
keyboards by Peter Bardens
(*above*, front row left), who later
made his name with Camel and
returned to play with Van on
Wavelength in 1978.

songwriter. The result was predictably patchy, neither great pop nor authentic-sounding rhythm and blues. "Gloria" was the only track that packed any punch.

Van felt burdened with everything going on around him. Unlike John Lennon or Mick Jagger he had no artistic equal within his own group who he could sharpen blades with, and his own songs – six of which were included – were not yet sufficiently polished.

"We'd worked on songs like 'Gloria' and we'd been playing 'Baby Please Don't Go' on stage, but when it came to the album it wasn't as if we were familiar with the stuff," explains Billy Harrison. "We had no time to improve the songs before we recorded. That's why a lot of it sounds very raw and similar, and as though there was not a lot going on."

The direction Van was to take in the future was indicated in songs such as "If You and I Could Be as Two", with its spoken introduction, and "Mystic Eyes", his first religious inference. The latter, which was to reach number 54 in the American charts, had started as a studio jam, and is the earliest recorded example of Van's technique of intonating a key phrase. His voice is first heard half-way through the 2½-minute song, and then after only four lines he takes the final line and repeats it seven times. "The lyrics were just words from another song I was writing at the time," said Van in October 1965. "We put it on tape the second time around."

On 11th June 1965 the eponymously titled album *Them* was released in Britain, with "Mystic Eyes" taken as the single. But again Them failed to set the charts on fire. There was growing resentment between the Solomons and the group, but Van – who was rapidly emerging as the front man – was reluctant to confront them. It was usually left to Billy Harrison to ask the awkward questions and this caused internal pressure, which finally led to the departure of Patrick John McAuley, Peter Bardens and Harrison himself. There was a short-lived but well-photographed line-up featuring Joe Boni on lead guitar and Terry Noone on drums. It lasted only a matter of weeks and never recorded.

Opposite: **A less than happy line-up of Them looking out of place at Ruislip Lido in August 1965. Guitarist Joe Boni (front) and drummer Terry Noone (behind Van) never recorded with the group.**

THEM

Van returned to Belfast to re-form Them after another internal shake-up. He recruited Ray Elliot (left) on keyboards, John Wilson (centre) on drums and lead guitarist Jim Armstrong (right).

Allthough Boni and Noone were only used as a temporary measure they featured in a lot of group photos during the summer of 1965 (*opposite & page 62*). The use of urban decay as a backdrop was meant to accentuate their image as young and tough rebels.

"As far as the Solomons were concerned the rest of the group didn't matter anyway," says Eric Wrixon. "They found Billy a bit too shrewd. He and I had been the only ones ever to try and find out what was going on financially, and when I left the band he had no support. He became a real thorn in their flesh, the only guy in the group forever asking to see statements."

Van and Alan Henderson, the only remaining members of the group, returned to Belfast to recruit new musicians, and to rehearse with them at the Maritime Hotel during the summer. By September the band was in place: Jim Armstrong from the Melotones on lead guitar, Ray Elliot from the Broadways on keyboards and John Wilson from the Misfits on drums.

On 24th September 1965 the newly re-formed Them played a 40-minute set at Belfast's Top Hat Club, before leaving for London. The local entertainment guide, *City Week*, called theirs "the most exciting sound to come out of the Ulster R & B movement".

"The fans fairly lapped it up even though some of the material . . . was very different from what they may have expected. There was an emphasis on soul jazz that would have raised an eyebrow if played by any other local group, but Them made such a job of it that most critics remained silent.

"The sight of Van Morrison and new boy Ray Elliot chase-chorusing their way through a two-tenor version of the Jimmy Giuffre/Bob Brookmeyer duet 'The Train and the River' would even have stimulated a Royal Showband fan who had arrived a night early at the hall."

The following week the group left for England and new recording dates with Decca. But the resulting single, "Call My Name", again failed to get them back in the charts.

The new line-up produced a far jazzier sound; while Ray Elliot tripled on flute, saxophone and vibes, Van was freer to experiment with his vocal improvisations.

"We had the power switched off at one gig because they were expecting aggressive rhythm and blues, and we were giving them something light and jazzy," remembers Jim Armstrong. "The management didn't like the new direction."

1321 K.ODAK

1321 K.ODAK

Van was now living in a rented flat in Notting Hill Gate, a cosmopolitan area of west London that was popular with students and immigrants and bordered on the more affluent Holland Park. He shared his flat with a girlfriend called Dee, who the rest of the group feared was an employee of the Solomons, put in position to control their charge. "She was a lot older than Van and she looked after him," says Armstrong. "She'd put his scarf on for him and give him money for his bottle of wine and his cigarettes."

In December 1965 Them recorded their second album, with Tommy Scott in total control. Phil Solomon was by this time no longer willing to pay for Bert Berns to come over to produce.

After the album was completed and before it was released in January 1966 under the title *Them Again*, there was yet another change of line-up. This time drummer John Wilson left to rejoin the Misfits and was replaced by David Harvey, to create the eighth incarnation of Them in two years.

Two months before their departure for America, the eighth line-up of Them, featuring new drummer David Harvey, performed an early-morning set on London's Embankment for American television.

CHAPTER FOUR

LOST
DREAMS
AND
FOUND
DREAMS
IN
AMERICA

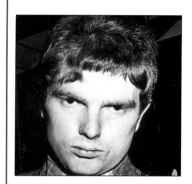

During a three-week stint at the prestigious Whiskey A-Go-Go club in Los Angeles (*left*), Them headlined over Captain Beefheart, the Association and the Doors. Van impressed Doors singer Jim Morrison, who later borrowed some of his stage moves and his best-known song, "Gloria".

AMERICA HAD BEEN A continual source of fascination and inspiration to Van since early childhood, and in May 1966 he visited for the first time, flying to San Francisco via New York for a two-month tour.

It was an opportune moment. The British beat-group invasion, which had been spearheaded by the Beatles and the Rolling Stones, was still in motion, the new West Coast bands were returning to blues and jazz roots, and Them's singles had been receiving a lot of airplay on FM radio in California, where they readily took to Van's "way out" lyrics (as the music trade magazine *Billboard* referred to them). The group had also scored three national hits in the summer of 1965, with "Baby Please Don't Go", "Here Comes the Night" and

"Mystic Eyes", and a re-released "Gloria" was climbing up the hot hundred.

Accompanied by producer Tommy Scott, who was representing Phil Solomon, they visited radio stations in San Francisco, before they flew down to Arizona for their American concert début in a giant football stadium, where they had to be driven across the pitch to reach the stage.

Their next shows were held in Los Angeles. They played a three-week stint at the 300-capacity Whiskey A-Go-Go Club on Sunset Boulevard, where they were supported at various times by Captain Beefheart and his Magic Band, the Association and the then unsigned Doors, who had a charismatic vocalist in Jim Morrison.

In his book *Riders on the Storm*, Doors bass player John Densmore recalls Van as a shy, insecure man who needed to drink heavily to gain the confidence to perform. He was impressed with the songs Van played him in private, and concluded that "it was as if he couldn't communicate on a small-talk party level, so he just burst into his songs".

Van's performances at the Whiskey A-Go-Go were ragged and violent, a mixture of inebriated wailing and rough-handling of the microphone stand. During some songs he would crouch low in front of the bass drum, a move that Jim Morrison was later to adopt.

A postcard of San Francisco (*above & below*) sent by Van from Los Angeles to Belfast rock journalist John Trew, commenting on a meeting with Bo Diddley, "a real head".

Right: Jim Armstrong, Van and Alan Henderson at the Whiskey A-Go-Go and (*pages 68–9*) with keyboard player Ray Elliot and drummer David Harvey.

COIT TOWER, SAN FRANCISCO
High atop Telegraph Hill is the towering Coit monument from which one may enjoy a panoramic view of all San Francisco.

C727

"I didn't understand why a guy with so much talent had to drink to get up on stage, or why he was so self-conscious up there," Densmore wrote. "The group was different, at least, I thought. It sure wasn't their performance; it was more their drunken, brawling foreign charisma. Jim [Morrison] thought they were great."

According to lead guitarist Jim Armstrong, even though they were only charged half-price at the bar, he and the other members of Them notched up a drinks bill of $2,600 during their first fortnight at the Whiskey. In addition Ray Elliot was visiting a liquor store in between sets, and coming back on stage with a coke can full of gin.

"At that stage Jim Morrison was a typical Californian grass-head, whereas we were from a drink background and were somewhat loath to take any of the other," says Armstrong. "So we started Jim on the drink really."

Although Van drank, he was not a party animal, and preferred to retire to his room at the Sunset Palms after the shows. As a result, Jim Morrison tended to socialise more with Elliot and Henderson, although he and Van distinguished themselves one night by being asked to leave a club for hurling abuse at the singer Johnny Rivers.

"Jim was much more of a raver," says Henderson. "I think he was possibly a bit jealous of Van's ability as a singer and writer because, at that time, the Doors weren't that good as a band."

From Los Angeles they travelled to San Francisco to play dates at the newly established Fillmore Auditorium, the Longshoremen's Hall and the Oakland Coliseum. On 23rd June, when playing at the Fillmore with the New Tweedy Brothers, Van met Janet Planet, the woman who was to become the inspiration for his best work and, eventually, his wife.

At the time Janet was a typical San Franciscan flower-child, with long brown hair, Victorian dresses and an interest in star signs. She was the first woman Van had met who seemed to understand his poetic soul, and when the group moved down to San Jose to play a residency at Losers South, Janet shared his room.

Already he had begun to translate his feelings for her into songs. "Ballerina", which was later to

The young Janet Planet, whom Van met while Them were playing in San Francisco, was the first woman to understand his mystically poetic ways. She was to become an enormous influence, later writing of his "essential core of aloneness [which] I had always feared could never be broken into".

So

Trying to make em friendly downtown
"Say who are you
Sell my soul what do you do

Trying to get across

Know the right place the right face
the right game the right name,
I'm on the dole trying to sell my
soul,
when where why and most of all how

Van was always to be seen scribbling lyrics on odd bits of paper. This is one that never made it into song, scrawled on the back of a notebook during a rehearsal with Them.

become a track on the *Astral Weeks* album, was almost certainly written to her at this time. Jim Armstrong remembers rehearsing it while on the tour, and playing it for the first time at the Waikiki Shell in Hawaii, during the group's brief visit to the island, where they shared a bill with the Ramsey Lewis Trio.

One of Van's rare comments about the song seems to confirm this. "I was in San Francisco one time in 1966 and I was attracted to the city," he said. "It was the first time I had been there, and I was sitting in this hotel and all these things were going through my head, and I had a flash about an actress in an opera house appearing in a ballet, and I think that's where the song came from." Janet Planet was an actress.

"Ballerina" was quite unlike anything he had written before. The chord pattern was simple but the dynamics were extraordinary. By altering the intensity of his voice he was able to create a mini-drama in seven minutes.

However, the American audiences wanted Them to be another Rolling Stones, and Van wasn't about to fulfil their expectations. This led to intense feelings of frustration that seemed to send him crazy. During a show in San Luis Obispo he finally lost his cool, and began to stalk Ray Elliot with a microphone stand.

"The band were cooking, it was a great gig but Van just freaked," remembers Jim Armstrong. "He was getting very funny on stage by this time. One night he would perform well and the next night he would just glower at the audience. The band was now huge on the West Coast and the crowds were screaming, but Van was going in a different direction and he couldn't cope with it."

After playing more dates in Arizona the tour ground to a halt in Los Angeles, when they were unable to extend their work visas. They were also by this time involved in a dispute with Phil Solomon over the accounting for the tour.

At the end of their run at the Whiskey they had been asked whether the cheque should be paid directly to them or to Solomon, and, out of curiosity more than anything else, they had asked for it to be made payable to the group. It turned out to be for $10,000 a week, whereas they had been asked to play for $2,000 a week minus a management fee of 35%. "We thought, hang on there," says Armstrong. "When we got to San Francisco we told Bill Graham that we wouldn't go on stage unless we got the money up front."

Phil Solomon does not disagree that they were getting a lot less than the American promoters were paying for them, but says that the group undertook the tour for an agreed fee rather than a percentage. "I gave them the guarantee," he says. "They then went to America and did good business, and then of course no longer wanted the guarantee. They wanted a percentage and so we split up."

Feelings between the two parties became bitter. According to Armstrong, the rupture in their relationship meant that the group's latest single, "Richard Cory", lost out on airplay. At the same time they were unable to extend their visas and so had to turn down offers of extra dates.

"It was a very bad time for all of us," says Armstrong. "We'd had a lot of success on the West Coast and then it all fell apart in an atmosphere of bitterness and acrimony."

At the end of the tour Van used some of his earnings to buy an expensive reel-to-reel tape recorder, and then flew back to London with Alan Henderson to make a last-ditch attempt to sort out business. Ray Elliot, Jim Armstrong and drummer David Harvey stayed on in Los Angeles.

They failed to reach an agreement with the Solomons and returned, dejected, to Belfast. Jim Armstrong, who had returned from America, and drummer Sammy Stitt joined Van and Henderson to play two last concerts, one in Derry and one in Dublin, before they decided to call it a day. Another version of Them, with Van replaced as vocalist by Kenny McDowell of the Mad Lads, did limp on.

With his new tape recorder installed at 125 Hyndford Street, where he was now living back with his parents, Van began writing more songs that followed the direction laid down by "Ballerina". He would play his guitar and improvise vocals until he hit a rich seam, which he would then mine for moods and images.

Two 45-minute sets jotted down by guitarist Jim Armstrong during tour rehearsals in Belfast.

He assembled a new band from the young musicians who hung around Crymbles Music Shop in the city centre on a Saturday afternoon. Mike Brown played bass, while Joe Hanratty played drums and Eric Bell, who was working with Shades of Blue, came in on guitar.

After playing through his set with them individually at home, he arranged for them to rehearse in a room over Dougie Knight's shop. The first show for the new group was at the opening night of the Square One Club in Royal Avenue.

A capacity crowd turned out that night to hear the new group billed as Van Morrison and Them Again. Alan Henderson turned up to double on bass for some Them numbers, such as "Mystic Eyes" and "Baby Please Don't Go", the local press were on hand and the room was so jammed that girls in the front were actually playing with the musicians' shoe laces.

"I had the list of the songs we were supposed to be playing on top of my amplifier," says Eric Bell. "Then Van looked at me and said, 'Start a blues in E, man.' I went, 'But what about the list?' He said, 'Fuck the list and start a blues in E, man.'

"So we all started playing this slow blues while Van played this blue Stratocaster that he'd hired from Crymbles and started just making things up as he went along. To me he was just like a jazz musician. That was his approach. He was inventing the lyrics as he sang, taking the volume right up and then bringing it right back down again."

On his return to Belfast after the American tour Van tried to resuscitate Them one last time, with a revamped line-up consisting of (left to right) Joe Hanratty (drums), Mike Brown (bass), Alan Henderson (bass), Eric Bell (lead guitar) and Van Morrison.

NEW THEM LINE-UP

THE THEM that opened up Royal Avenue's SQUARE ONE last weekend. The kooky guy in the bottom right corner is Van the Morrison who looks even kookier in his wee blue cloak.

On the left is ex-Alleykatz bass Mike Brown who is/was with the Silhouettes. At the back is another Alleykat—Joe Hanratty—who drummed.

Looking happy in the middle is Alan Henderson —who turned up giving the group a second bass. And at the end — Eric 'Slowhand' Bell—late of the Castaways and Unit and now leading THEM.

The group plays yet another gig together in Carrickfergus Town Hall to-morrow when they top the bill to the Bangor Carpetbaggers and the Fugitives in a beat-feast . . . It should be a helluva night 'cos Carrick seems to be switching on towards beat this winter.

Frankie 'Styx' Connolly got pulled offstage twice in the Town Hall last weekend . . . heaven knows what they'll do to poor Van!

Their next performance was at Carrickfergus Town Hall, where Van turned a few heads by arriving in a floral suit that he'd bought in San Francisco. His behaviour now appeared quite erratic to the other members of the group. He wasn't letting them know which songs he was planning to do, and was starting songs on his own. "Then, in the middle of the set, he asked for the volume to be turned down while he walked to the microphone with a big book in his hand," says Bell. "He stood there and said, 'To wank to not to wank, that is the question.' I was speechless! Then he repeated it in exactly the same way.

"When he didn't seem to be getting much of a reaction he said, 'Hands up all the wankers in the hall.' There were still Teddy boys around in Belfast in those days, and a few of them didn't like it at all, and they started throwing pennies on the stage, and the promoter had to clamber up and appeal for calm. I know we all went home early that night. Van was obviously out of his head."

The group played a few more local gigs, at Sammy Houston's Jazz Club and at Queen's University, but it was obvious that Van had outgrown his original audience. By early 1966 he was playing more sax on stage and taking off into bursts of lyrical improvisation.

"I think he was a bit pissed off at being back in Belfast," says Bell. "It obviously wasn't the same vibe as in America . . . It was about 300 years behind the times as far as he was concerned."

During this period he had been writing a lot more songs with the use of the new tape recorder, and sending tracks to record companies. Philips in London had begun to show some interest and also Bert Berns, who was now running a label called Bang in New York.

In March, Herbie Armstrong, who was now playing guitar in a four-piece band with Brian Rossi called the Wheels, asked Van if he would like to join. "I can remember standing with him outside a fish and chip shop in the Creggah Road," remembers Herbie. "He told me that he was very keen to come over to join the Wheels, but that he had a phone call to make to Bert Berns in America."

When Van arrived back home after the American tour he seemed more restless than ever. Belfast could no longer contain him and he was eager to find a sympathetic audience. "Just as we were starting to grow our hair long he had cut all his off," remembers guitarist Eric Bell. "It was as if everything we were trying to do he had already done."

The phone call confirmed that Berns was keen to team up with him again. Dougie Knight remembers Van coming into his shop, and announcing very matter-of-factly that he was going to be making a record in New York.

"He never actually boasted about things," says Knight. "He simply stated things and did it in such an undramatic way that you couldn't take him very seriously. Then, of course, within a matter of days the word was out that he'd signed a contract and was in America."

Berns's plan was to record four singles, including both A and B sides, over a two-day period with a group of session musicians. Van flew to New York where the first session took place on 28th March 1966, at A & R Recording Studios on 112 West 48th Street.

On "Brown-eyed Girl", which was finally captured on the 22nd take, Berns achieved a satisfying balance between his own pop instincts and Van's adherence to rhythm and blues. "Ro Ro Rosey" and "Goodbye Girl", also both recorded on the first day, were less successful attempts at a single.

"TB Sheets" was an emotional $9\frac{1}{2}$-minute rap about a friend's dying days in hospital. It would never have made it as a single, but was presumably an indulgence allowed by Berns. The musicians had obviously been told to set up a riff while Van unspooled his emotions, and discovered what he felt as the words came tumbling out.

Van has never commented on who the dying "Julie" was, but he would later introduce the song on stage as being about a real person. Brooks Arthur, the engineer on the session, recalls him literally breaking down in tears in the vocal booth after it had been recorded. "He was just torn apart," says Arthur. "He was sitting on the floor in a heap like a wrung-out dishcloth, completely spent emotionally."

The following day Van returned to record another four tracks: "Who Drove the Red Sports Car", "Midnight Special", "Spanish Rose" and "He Ain't Give You None". In addition to a clear lack of direction – Berns apparently pulled towards pop while Van experimented with Dylanesque impressions – both sessions were hampered by a leaden musical approach. "I think it should be freer, you know? We should have a free thing going," Van is heard to say as he stops the band on an early take of "He Ain't Give You None". "At the minute we have a choke thing going. You know what I mean?"

The next day Van was on the plane back to Belfast and an uncertain future. He was to keep a low profile over the next three months, during which he spent a lot of his time at home on Hyndford Street, writing most of the songs that would make up *Astral Weeks*.

"Ballerina" was already in the bag, and "Madame George" and "Beside You" were among the first songs written during this period. "Astral Weeks" itself is clearly a song written to Janet Planet, the girl he had left behind on "the far side of the ocean", but who he was trusting to bring about his rebirth, "in another time/In another place". The lines about "taking care of your boy" referred to Janet's young son Peter, who she was raising alone.

As with the best of his songs, "Astral Weeks" combined concrete imagery with an otherworldly yearning. The rebirth could be a new career, a new life in America, or it could be a spiritual transformation, the assurance of a "home on high". It could refer to both, for now Van was dredging up ideas and phrases buried deep in his Irish consciousness, and coupling them with contemporary observations.

"I think it just changed to coming from a deeper unconscious level," he later said of these songs. "It was more to do with getting in touch with the unconscious."

"Brown-eyed Girl" was Van's first single to be released on the Bang label, and it made an unexpectedly high showing in the American hit parade, entering the *Cashbox* charts on 22nd July and eventually rising to number 8 (10 in the *Billboard* charts).

With a hit on his hands Berns rapidly made plans to have his star returned to America. Van was brought to New York and set up in a hotel opposite Berns's offices at 1650 Broadway, while promotional plans were set in motion. Janet and Peter flew in from California to move in with Van.

A band composed of Eric Oxendine on bass, Bob

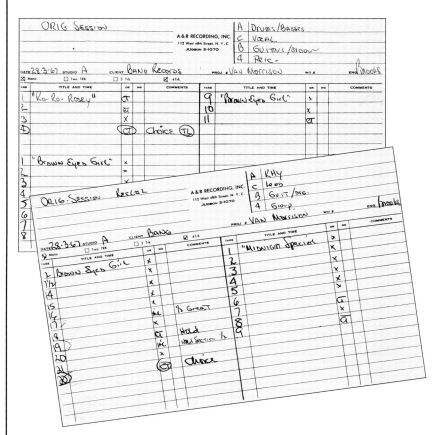

Above: Session sheets from Van's first recordings with Bert Berns's Bang label in New York reveal that they took place in a two-day period in March 1967 and that "Brown-eyed Girl", his first hit single in America under his own name, was perfected on the 22nd take. *Below*: Back in America, Van was reunited with Janet, who moved in with him at his Manhattan hotel with her young son Peter.

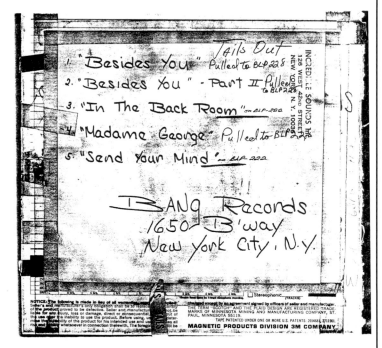

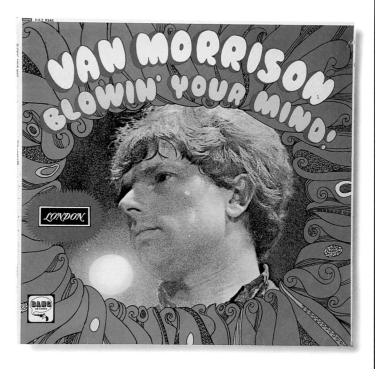

Van always disowned *Blowin' Your Mind* and shortly after its release began recording tracks like "Madame George" (seen on tape box of master) which would eventually lead to *Astral Weeks*. Van was launched by Bang on a boat trip on the Hudson river, where he played an energetic set (*opposite*).

Grenier on drums and Charlie Brown on guitar was formed to support Van as he made showcase appearances in clubs, and on radio and television. Berns hired a boat for a celebration party that cruised up and down the Hudson river, while champagne corks popped and music business hangers-on crowded around the new Irish star.

But Van did not seem to appreciate the attention. The unco-operative and moody tendencies that had been observed since childhood surfaced with a vengeance.

Bang didn't know how to handle him. They were hoping for a bright new pop star and found themselves with a temperamental Irish poet who wouldn't be squeezed into a mould.

"Through his behaviour he gave Bert a lot of trouble," says Berns's wife Eileen. "He was out of control. Bert got him some appearances in Greenwich Village where the press were invited along, and the only way to describe the way he behaved in front of them is to say that he was unprofessional. He made life very difficult for Bang."

The antagonism between Van and Berns intensified when, in order to capitalise on the success of "Brown-eyed Girl", Bang put out an album of the eight songs that had been recorded in March, dressed it up in a neo-psychedelic jacket and titled it *Blowin' Your Mind*.

Van was incensed, not only because he hadn't been informed (he learned of its release while on the road), but because he considered the tracks unfinished, and hated the implication given by the packaging that he was a part of the love and drugs trend.

In order to pacify his artist Berns suggested that they cut a proper album, and, with this in mind, they returned to A & R Studios in November to record a further eight tracks. The result again wavered between the outrageously pop ("Chick-A-Boom") and the embarrassingly obscure ("It's All Right"); the best track was "Beside You", which was to be re-recorded the following year for *Astral Weeks*. An unpolished "Madame George" was also taped, with party sounds mixed in.

All in all it was not a very inspiring session, and the results sounded more like rough demos than final cuts. Van had not yet mastered the technique of composing at the microphone, which meant that

Van called his *Best of . . .* album **The Worst of Van Morrison** claiming it was sabotaged by producer Bert Berns (*opposite*, to the left of Van and Janet). It led to a rift between producer and artist, and Van moved to Woodstock with his bass player Tom Kielbania (*page 82*).

some of the lyrics seemed banal and were delivered with fake brashness.

Bang had the effrontery to title the finished product *The Best of Van Morrison*, but Van was not flattered. He knew he hadn't realised the sound that was going through his head. "It should have been called *The Worst of . . .*," he later admitted. "When I started I was told I would be able to do my own thing, but then it got sabotaged. I actually redid some of the songs on *Astral Weeks* just to show how they really should be done."

The relationship between Berns and Van had now completely soured, then on 30th December 1967 Berns died suddenly of a heart attack. Eileen took over the company, but it was clear that Van would not be continuing as a Bang artist.

He was already being courted by some of the major record labels and Joe Smith, then President of Warner Brothers Records, arranged to sort out his Bang contract. An agreement was reached, according to which Van would be free to leave the label in return for the publishing rights to his next ten tracks.

"He then turned over a tape to me that he must have spent a few minutes making," remembers Eileen Berns. "It consisted of ten bursts of nonsense music that weren't even really songs. You could never have copyrighted them. There was something about ringworms and then he sang something about 'I gotta go in and cut this stupid song for this stupid lady' and so on.

"To cut a long story short, I had two small babies, one of them born three weeks before Bert's death, and I just wanted to get on with my life, and so I didn't bother to take him to court and sue him over the songs I didn't get. So I just let it go."

Van left for Cambridge, Massachusetts, to begin a new life with Janet in an apartment on Green Street, a low-rent area that was popular with hippies and students, and lay midway between Harvard University and the Massachusetts Institute of Technology (MIT). After settling in he formed an electric band that included Charlie Marriano on saxophone and Tom Kielbania from the Berkeley School of Music on bass, and they began to play in modest clubs and college halls in the immediate area.

His one great champion at the time was Peter Wolf, a 21-year-old rhythm and blues enthusiast, who was the singer with a local band, the Hallucinations (later to become the J. Geils Band), as well as an all-night disc jockey on Boston's top FM radio station WCBN. Wolf promoted Van heavily through his radio show and also put him in touch with a local promoter.

In mid-1968 Van decided to go for an acoustic sound, and sacked all of his band except Kielbania, who by this time was playing an upright bass. It was during this short period of working as part of a duo and then a trio, with the addition of flautist John Payne, that he arrived at the sound that would eventually define his album *Astral Weeks*.

Payne, a 22-year-old philosophy student at Harvard, met Van at the Catacombs Club in Boston after being introduced by Kielbania. A jazz musician by training, he had little idea of who Van was and was initially unimpressed by what he heard.

"I listened through the first set and then Van asked me to join him for the second," Payne remembers. "As soon as I stood there and started playing with him I could feel what he was trying to do. It was only when he played 'Brown-eyed Girl' that I realised who he was and what I was dealing with.

"After that show he asked me if I'd come back the next night and then asked me if I'd join him. I said, sure. I dropped out fast from Harvard and went down to New York where he was planning to make a new album."

The new album was to be *Astral Weeks*.

Above: a drawing of Van made in 1965 by his artist friend Cezil McCartney. *Left:* Van at the Bang launch with Jeff Barry, a friend of Bert Berns who sang backing vocals on some *Blowin' Your Mind* tracks.

CHAPTER FIVE

ASTRAL WEEKS

The long-haired, poetic-looking Van dressed in a floral shirt was the image that was to accompany *Astral Weeks*, the album destined to establish him as one of rock's most creative forces.

LEGEND HAS IT THAT *Astral Weeks* was recorded in two eight-hour sessions with virtually no overdubs, but the truth, while not contradicting the essential spontaneity of the project, is slightly different.

Van and Janet, whom he had secretly married, moved down to New York with Tom Kielbania and John Payne to prepare for Van's first album to be recorded with Warner Brothers. Despite his ill-fated relationships with Phil Solomon and Bert Berns, Van had entered into yet another complicated deal, this time with Inherit Productions, who were described as "a division of Schwaid-Merenstein".

Schwaid-Merenstein was Bob Schwaid and Lew Merenstein, a little-known entrepreneurial duo, whose main claim to fame had been managing South African singer Miriam Makeba. Van was signed to Inherit Productions who, in turn, had signed a contract to produce two albums with Warner Brothers Records. It was intended that Schwaid would hire the musicians and organise the sessions while Merenstein, who had worked as a studio engineer, would produce the tracks.

Warner Brothers didn't want to overspend on sessions that sprawled over weeks or months, and so Schwaid was urged to minimise the margin of error by recruiting the best New York session musicians available. This Schwaid undeniably did. In order to build on the acoustic jazz feel that Van had been developing with Payne and Kielbania, he booked some of the best-qualified jazz players working in the city: guitarist Jay Berliner (who had played with Charles Mingus on *The Black Saint & the Sinner Lady*), bassist Richard Davis (who had worked with Miles Davis), percussionist Warren Smith Jr and Modern Jazz Quartet drummer Connie Kay.

One evening in September 1968, along with arranger Larry Fallon, they gathered in Century Sound, a studio on West 52nd Street owned by Brooks Arthur, who had engineered the Bang sessions, ready to work on Van's new material. Payne and Kielbania, who were still members of Van's band, were considered too inexperienced and had to content themselves with watching from the control room.

Van has since said that the songs on *Astral Weeks* were written to a story-line, but that Merenstein had them placed out of sequence on the finished album. The cover description of "In the Beginning" for the first side and "Afterwards" for the second he claimed had no significance.

In a later interview he complained that "I was kind of restricted [during the making of the album] because it wasn't really understood what I really wanted." This came as a surprise to the musicians who played on the album as they remember him as being distinctly uncommunicative, never discussing the sound he wanted or giving any clue as to what the songs were about. "He seemed spaced out," remembers John Payne. "He appeared as though he was in a lot of personal pain." None of the hired people had any idea of who Van was and, even if they had known of his reputation, it would hardly have made any impression on musicians more used to playing with the likes of Mingus and Miles.

"Ironically, the image that you have when you listen to the album now is of these guys who are all together, and they realise that they are creating a monumental work of art," says Payne, "but the fact was that this was just another session for them.

Although Van was never a user of psychedelic drugs, *Astral Weeks*, with its surreal moments and its suggestion of spiritual rebirth, was often regarded as embodying "the sound of acid".

Drummer Connie Kay and bass
player Richard Davis were to
give *Astral Weeks* its distinctive
light jazz flavour. They were
recruited initially because it was
feared that rock musicians would
spend too long on the sessions
and Warner Brothers were keen
to keep down expenditure.

"The only guy who really looked as though he was getting into it was Jay Berliner. I'm not saying that they were all just sitting there thinking, another day, another dollar, but I couldn't say for sure that they weren't."

There was no rehearsal before the first session, just a brief run-through by Van and chord charts prepared by Larry Fallon issued to the band. The idea was that they would start playing and get into a groove. The editing would take place at a later stage.

"These guys just jammed together," says Tom Kielbania, who showed Richard Davis the bass lines he had been using with Van. "They went right through those songs and then cut all the solos out. If they hadn't done that every track would have been the whole side of an album!"

The first three songs they recorded were "Beside You", "Cyprus Avenue" and "Madame George". Drummer Connie Kay wasn't used on the first session but instead an uncredited flautist, who looked bored throughout the proceedings, was brought in. John Payne, believing he could do better, pestered Merenstein throughout the day to be allowed a chance to play.

"After three songs they decided they had done what they wanted for that day but Merenstein said, well, everybody's feeling good so why don't we do one more song?" he remembers. "He turned to me and said, why don't you play? I hadn't even brought my flute, so I had to ask the other guy if I could use his. He let me and I played on 'Astral Weeks'. It was the first time I had heard the song and it was the first time I had recorded with Van; I was the flute player on the album from then on.

"Van never discussed the song. He never talked about anything. The ending sounds rehearsed but it was the first and only take. I can remember Larry Fallon walking out and saying, we don't have a chord chart for this. But that was the only take and they named the album after it."

Van's performance had been transformed since the final Bang sessions of the previous year. His voice sounded stronger and more confident, the lyrics were more carefully honed and the musical setting was perfectly in keeping with his aspirations. Engineer Brooks Arthur, who had witnessed the change first hand, remembers it as a time when

Eccentric Irish painter Cezil McCartney, who sketched Van in 1965 and 1966, introduced him to arcane literature and was an influence on the titling of *Astral Weeks*. "A friend of mine had drawings in his flat of astral projection," Van told me. "I was at his house when I was working on a song which began 'If I venture down the slipstream' and that's why I called it *Astral Weeks*."

Although only a few minutes' walk from Hyndford Street, the wide sweep of Cyprus Avenue with its large detached houses seemed like another world to the young Van Morrison. On *Astral Weeks* he wrote of its being a place where he had experienced childhood raptures which he came to believe were of a spiritual nature.

electricity flowed in the studio: "Van was much more in control than he had been before, yet there was also trepidation on his part because it was his first step away from Bang. I think his confidence grew as the sessions went on."

The next session was scheduled for early in the morning, possibly the following day, but for some reason things didn't work out as well and nothing from it was ever used. "It just didn't happen," says Payne. "It was the wrong time of day for jazz musicians to create. I think that by the end of that session we all knew that nothing was going to be used. They just said, let's forget it."

For the final session they again came together in the evening, and quickly found themselves back in the same groove. "There's a certain feel about a seven-to-ten-o'clock session," Richard Davis recently told *Rolling Stone* magazine. "You've just come back from a dinner break, some guys have had a drink or two, it's this dusky part of the day, and everybody's relaxed. Sometimes that can be a problem, but with this record, I remember that the ambience of that time of day was all through everything we played."

They completed the album with "Slim Slow Slider", "Ballerina", "Sweet Thing" and "Young Lovers Do", during which they again jammed for extended periods. "Slim Slow Slider", the closing track on the album, was one long improvisation that had its middle section snipped out.

"Van was improvising vocally and Richard Davis and I were improvising on our instruments," recalls Payne. "It was unbelievable. It made me sick that they cut it out. There's a splice right near the end of the song which you can hear if you listen to the album. Immediately after Van sings 'I don't know what to do' you hear the bass player hitting his stuff, and that's where the ten minutes was cut out."

"Slim Slow Slider" was a first take that everyone had believed to be only a sound-check. Merenstein had suggested that everyone stop playing except Van, Davis and Payne on soprano sax. "They managed to get a sound on my sax where it sounds half-way between a sax and a flute," says Payne. "It sounds as if it's coming across a lake."

In February 1969 Van Morrison moved to Woodstock, New York State, to get away from the world. Six months later the world started coming to Woodstock.

A week later strings and horns were overdubbed, again at Century Sound. It was also at this time that the harpsichord was added to "Cyprus Avenue". According to Payne, Van was much more forthcoming with suggestions at these sessions.

The result, released in November 1968, was one of the most stunningly original albums ever recorded in the rock genre, although its originality actually lay in its distance from anything vaguely rock. There was no electric guitar or bass, no thudding drums and no piano or organ. The two most vital instruments were the acoustic bass of Richard Davis, which sensitively wove around the moods of the songs, and Van's voice, which through modulation and invocation exploited the hidden depths of every word he'd written. As American music critic Lester Bangs wrote a decade later: "Van Morrison is interested, obsessed, with how much musical or verbal information he can compress into a small space, or picture."

Many years later, when asked why he had started writing mystical songs, Van pointed out that *Astral Weeks* was "probably the most spiritually lyrical album I've ever done". He was right in that it was essentially an album about rebirth that stated the themes of love, childhood, ecstatic experience and personal transformation which have preoccupied him ever since.

"It sounded like the man who made *Astral Weeks* was in terrible pain, pain most of Van Morrison's previous works had only suggested," wrote Bangs. "But like the later albums by the Velvet Underground, there was a redemptive element in the blackness, ultimate compassion for the suffering of others, and a swathe of pure beauty and mystical awe that cut right through the heart of the work."

For many people at the time *Astral Weeks* perfectly articulated the experience of the acid trip, with its invocation to be born again and its subsequent journey through layers of childhood experience in flashback sequences. It became one of the essential albums for travellers on the "hippie trail" from Europe through to Kathmandu, and there were even reports of vans painted in psychedelic colours being renamed "the Van Morrison".

Yet in my interview with Van in 1985 he denied ever having taken LSD. "I always thought it very strange [that *Astral Weeks* became a favourite album for acid-heads]," he said. "I always told people that I was definitely anti-drugs and I've been anti-drugs for a long time . . . I didn't need drugs to have experiences. I had always had experiences without drugs, and so anything like that would impair them. Alcohol would impair them. It produces a false ecstasy."

Friends confirm that he didn't indulge in acid, and had a great fear that someone would spike his drinks. He was, however, known to take amphetamines and to smoke marijuana, and implicitly acknowledged this in 1974 when he claimed that he had given up drugs in 1970 because "I just got tired of doing it so I stopped. It wasn't doing anything for me any more."

He told at least one friend that he blamed the irregularity of his career in the late sixties on the impairing quality of these drugs. He felt that they had been responsible for his losing control over both his business and his art.

Astral Weeks has won so many plaudits over the past twenty-five years, as one of the ten most influential albums of the rock era, that it is often forgotten that it was never a hit album and that its total US sales to date are barely more than 250,000. However, Joe Smith, Warners' president at the time of its release, took a long-term view when he stated – in what would then have been considered very optimistic terms – that *Astral Weeks* was the sort of album that would still be selling in six years' time.

Surprisingly Van did not share a lot of the enthusiasm because he felt it lacked variation. "The arrangements are too samey," he told musician Happy Traum in an interview in 1970. "Guys like Richard Davis and Jay Berliner have got a distinctive style and they're groovy for like two songs . . . but four or five other songs should have had a change in mood. That should have happened, and it didn't."

Despite his fine creation and the respect he was earning from his peers and the music critics, he was in dire financial straits and looking for any dates he could get to bring in cash. At times he was reduced

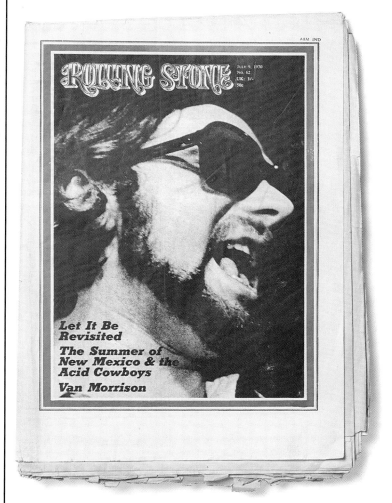

In July 1970 he made the cover of *Rolling Stone*. He was interviewed at length by folk musician Happy Traum.

to playing unpaid guest spots in New York clubs, and found himself supporting acts like Tim Hardin, Moby Grape and Rhinosaurus.

The lack of live work did not mean that Van slackened the pace. He insisted that Payne and Kielbania turned up at Merenstein's office each day for a back-room rehearsal. Already homesick for Boston and his new wife, Payne decided that he was not going to stay in New York to attend a string of never-ending rehearsals, and so he left the band.

His replacement was found in British-born Graham "Monk" Blackburn, and it was he who persuaded Van and Kielbania to move with him to Woodstock, in upstate New York. "I didn't really want to live in the city anyway," says Blackburn. "Van was very keen on the idea because he was a big fan of The Band who were living in Woodstock at the time, and he knew that I was friends with them."

In February 1969 Woodstock was still a sleepy settlement in the Catskill Mountains that attracted painters, sculptors and musicians who wanted to live close to New York City but away from the dust and grime.

Blackburn found Van and Janet a house to rent on Oyaho Mountain, and then introduced Van to The Band, most of whom were at the time living in a house nicknamed Big Pink in nearby West Saugerties. "I remember that they were kind of bemused by Van's apparent adulation, because they thought he was just as respected and famous as they were," says Blackburn. "Bob Dylan was also living on Ohayo Mountain, but I don't think he and Van really knew each other at that time."

Life at last seemed more settled and those who visited Van and Janet saw them as a close, loving couple. "She was a very happy-go-lucky girl," says Tom Kielbania. "She seemed optimistic about everything. He could get depressed but she was exactly the opposite."

John Payne, who also saw the couple in Woodstock, agrees: "She was very sweet. She worshipped him artistically and yet I couldn't figure out how she put up with him. She was very calm. She was totally devoted to Van and his career and to believing in him."

Van Morrison and Janet Planet married in 1968, and their early days together in Woodstock were among their happiest (*above & overleaf*). "Janet was always very optimistic about everything," remembers bass player Tom Kielbania. "She used to keep Van going."

In July 1969 Kielbania left to get married. It was one month before the Woodstock Festival would arrive to shatter the community's rural isolation for ever (even though the festival actually took place over fifty miles away). Frustrated by the lack of live work Blackburn also left later in the year.

The Colwell-Winfields Blues Band, who Van knew from Boston, were also resident in Woodstock at the time and on the point of breaking up, so Van recruited from them, and took with him bass player John Klingberg, and horn players Colin Tillton and Jack Schroer. Van's road manager, an English travel agent living in Woodstock, came across guitarist John Platania playing in a local club and recommended him as a further member.

With the new band Van returned to A & R Studios in New York to record *Moondance*, the first album he was to both produce and arrange. Although he was still under contract to Inherit Productions, Lew Merenstein was described quite pointedly as "executive producer" on the album sleeve, an indication that all was not well between the two parties.

Moondance was a more joyous and relaxed album than *Astral Weeks*, and fulfilled Van's aim of producing a record that wasn't "samey". He introduced a horn section and backing vocals, which allowed him to swing from Stax-like soul to cocktail-bar jazz and country blues. It was much more a collection of songs than a single statement, and marked his commercial breakthrough as a solo artist. It would produce a top forty single, "Come Running", and go on to become his first million-selling album.

If *Astral Weeks* was the result of inspiration, then *Moondance* was the result of perspiration. The lyrics were obviously worked at rather than grabbed from the subconscious, and when laid out on the page look more structured.

The apparent effortlessness of the title track was achieved only after repeated attempts throughout 1969 to tape a version that satisfied him. Graham Blackburn reckons that during his time with Van they must have made at least six visits to New York to record the song. "It seemed as though every other week we were in the studio recording 'Moondance'," he says. "Van likes to be spontaneous in the studio,

Although *Astral Weeks* was the album that won him the greatest critical acclaim, it was *Moondance* that made the big commercial breakthrough, reaching number 32 in the US album charts. The proof sheets (*opposite & page 100*) are from Elliott Landy's cover shoot.

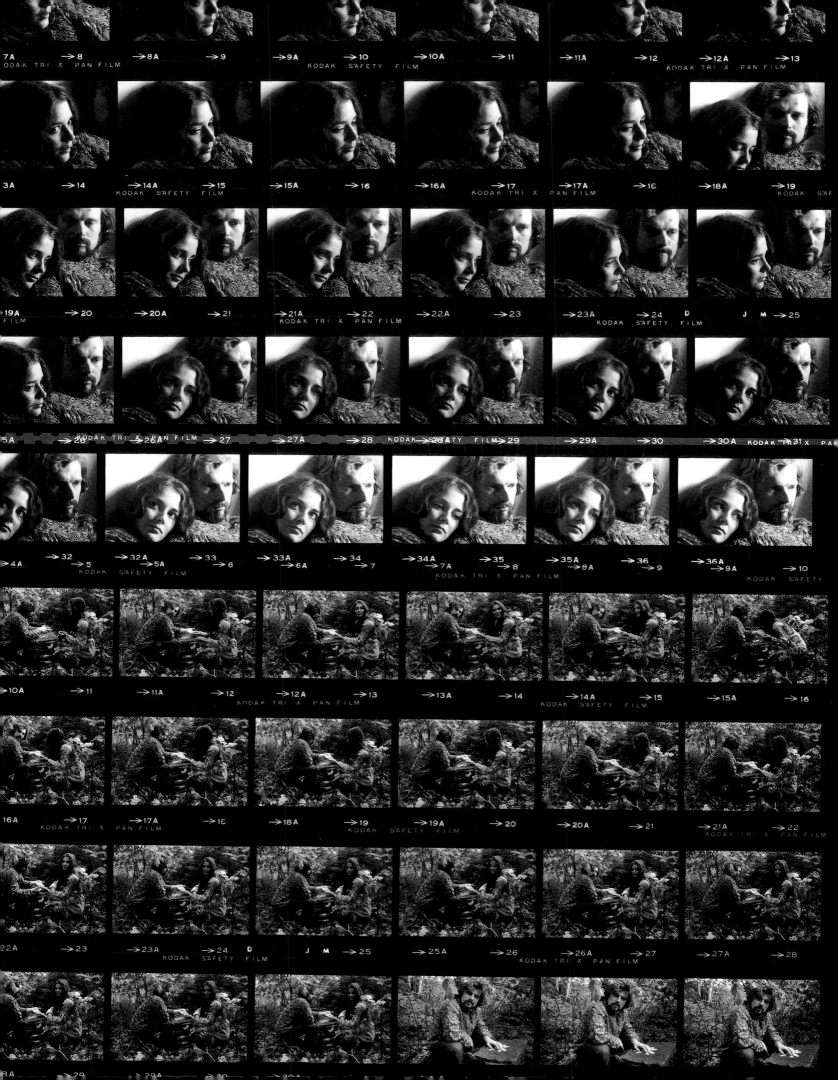

but it's a spontaneity that he has to wait a long time to achieve, while you are sitting around waiting for instructions.

"He would try and get himself in the mood and get a groove going, but then at the end of it he'd say, it's not right, it's not right. No one knew what was going on. We'd all be pulling our hair out and then we'd have to do it all over again."

The influence of The Band, whose first album *Music from Big Pink* had been released in August 1968, was evident in songs such as "And It Stoned Me" and "Caravan". "Brand New Day" was a response to his first hearing their version of Dylan's biblically-inspired "I Shall Be Released".

The album's classic track was "Into the Mystic", a celebration of mystical union that he once stated was about "being part of the universe". It combined all his main themes: nature (sun, sea, wind, sky), a lover, the yearning for things to be as they were in "the days of old", the foghorn sounds of Belfast and the promise of redemption through unity with the whole.

It also brought together his developing musical themes, beginning almost as a folk tune, with an acoustic guitar, and rising to a crescendo of soul music, with horns introduced on the chorus. On the line "And I want to rock your gypsy soul", he displayed his ability to create poetry in performance out of otherwise mundane collections of words.

Although he later claimed that the original lyric had been "into the misty" (just as "Madame George" had originally been "Madame Joy"), it was this song more than any other that encouraged the word "mystic" to be so frequently applied to him. In 1987 he claimed it to be "the most mystical song I've ever written". But the exact nature of his mystical experience was none too clear, for he never discussed his spiritual beliefs with those who worked with him, and no one who knew him at the time would have described him as religious.

Moondance was an album of new beginnings. Both his marriage and his new recording career had obviously brought him a degree of satisfaction, and this was reflected in the new collection of songs.

He appeared to idolise Janet, and saw her not merely as a lover, but as a saviour. When he sang that her loving "makes me righteous, it makes me

Woodstock had for many years been a refuge for artists, writers and musicians. Here Van is embraced by Clarence, a sculptor who lived nearby on Ohayo Mountain and who had constructed a home out of reclaimed garbage.

The gatefold sleeve of *His Band and the Street Choir* presented the image of a Van Morrison at peace with himself and in love with the world. The songs inside told a different story.

whole", he was consciously using the image of religious redemption.

In "And It Stoned Me" he again referred to one of his childhood experiences of wonder that was to inspire his soul-searching. It has often been regarded as an example of nature mysticism, but as Van explained to me in 1985, it was written about an experience he had as a child. "I suppose I was about twelve years old," he said. "We used to go to a place called Ballystockert to fish. We stopped in the village on the way up to this place and I went to this little stone house, and there was an old man there with dark weather-beaten skin, and we asked him if he had any water.

"He gave us some water which he said he'd got from the stream. We drank some and everything seemed to stop for me. Time stood still. For five minutes everything was really quiet and I was in this 'other dimension'. That's what the song is about."

While in Woodstock his relationship with Janet began to deteriorate. "He was still completely in love with her," remembers John Platania, "but it was definitely becoming strained. There were dramas all the time."

His Band and the Street Choir, recorded early in 1970, reflected his diminishing hope. Although it is still largely an album of love songs, there is an imploring quality about it. It is apparent that he feels that his love, who, after all, has been the inspiration for his best work, may be drifting out of reach.

In "Give Me a Kiss" he assures his woman that he wants only "one more kiss", in "If I Ever Needed Someone" he begs for "someone to hold on to/To keep me from all fear", and in "I'll Be Your Lover" he begs her to reach out for him, "so that I'll be the one/ Who's always reaching out for you".

The following year a daughter, Shana, was born to the couple, but it was too late to stop the drift. Just as everything seemed to be coming together for Van, everything was starting to fall apart.

CHAPTER SIX

SOME-TIMES IT GETS SO HARD

This Warner Brothers publicity photo typified the period and cast Van as a hippy troubadour.

IN APRIL 1971 VAN left Woodstock. The owner of the house he was renting wanted to move back in, he later explained, and the documentary film *Woodstock* (released the previous year) had altered the spirit of the small community and made it a magnet for gawpers and gazers, who expected to walk through its streets and catch sight of Bob Dylan shopping, or Jimi Hendrix walking his dog.

"When I first went, people were moving there to get away from the scene," he told Richard Williams of *Melody Maker*. "Then Woodstock itself started being the scene. Everybody and his uncle started showing up at the bus station, and that was the complete opposite of what it was supposed to be."

Yet Van was unlikely to have been affected by these pressures, because his home was remote and he wasn't noted for socialising in Woodstock's cafés and bars. If he had wanted to stay he could easily have found alternative accommodation. John Platania believes it was domestic pressure that eventually prompted his departure. "He didn't want to leave but Janet wanted to move out West," he says. "He was manipulated into going."

Janet was a woman who loved the sunshine and wanted to return to California where her family still lived, and so Van reluctantly picked up sticks and moved to Inverness, north of Marin County, where he bought a beautiful hilltop home surrounded by redwood trees.

He seemed by now to have slipped into a cosy domestic routine. In a rare interview at the time, Janet told Ireland's *New Spotlight* magazine that Van didn't like socialising or performing. She said it without any hint of malice, but it was an indication of the tensions building up between them.

"Really he is a recluse," she said. "He is quiet. We never go anywhere. We don't go to parties. We never go out. We have an incredibly quiet life and going on the road is the only excitement we have." What she really meant was that he only really came alive with his music, and whereas this was wonderful for his audience it was wearing on a partner.

"Janet wanted to get into acting but Van wanted a traditional woman at home and I know that bothered her," says John Platania. "At that point she was so young and just wanted to step out on her own. "She controlled a lot of his musical direction. She had a big, big influence on him. She sang backing vocals for him, helped him choose material, offered business advice. She was a strong person. People used to offer her modelling assignments and acting roles, but Van flatly refused to allow her to do these things. The lack of socialising drove her crazy."

Yet these tensions were barely discernible to those who bought his albums, because *Tupelo Honey* – written in Woodstock but recorded in San Francisco – was presented as an expression of rural bliss; the cover photograph showed Janet on horseback trotting through a sun-dappled glade, while her husband dutifully walked alongside.

When Van and Janet moved to Marin County, California, with their daughter Shana and Janet's son Peter, the tensions in their relationship came to the surface.

A cursory listen to the songs appeared to confirm this harmonious picture, as Van sang heartily of the good life at home with his "woman". But closer inspection of the songs revealed that all was obviously not well. His pain and anguish were apparent for he wrote as if his introverted nature was losing him his lover. In "I Wanna Roo You", he portrayed what to him was obviously a good night's entertainment. His woman is in the kitchen cooking, he's angling for a bit of late-night seduction and he comments, "Ain't going no-where/And we don't have many friends," apparently oblivious of the fact that this might not have been the social life his wife desired. Even in "You're My Woman" there was a tinge of desperation. The words were strong – she was his "sunshine" and he was her "guiding light" – but they sounded more like stiff reminders than celebrations.

Tupelo Honey was produced by Van with assistance from Ted Templeman, and the working routine was to aim for as live a sound as possible. The vocals were always live.

"We'd have rehearsals beforehand in which we'd go through each song five or six times," remembers saxophonist Boots Houston. "Then when we went into the studio we would just play a whole set straight through without repeating anything.

"We would have played maybe twenty songs and Van would go back and cut out the songs he didn't want. The only time we'd go back would be to overdub backing vocals or horns."

The end result, released in November 1971, went into *Billboard*'s top thirty, but again Van had reservations. "I wasn't very happy with that album," he said. "It wasn't really fresh. It was a whole bunch of songs that had been hanging around for a while . . . I never really listened to it much. I've got a bad taste in my mouth for both *Street Choir* and *Tupelo Honey*."

Despite the country and family image surrounding this period, in retrospect Van sees it as "intense" rather than laid back. He was contracted to produce two albums a year, was under pressure to produce chart singles and, since moving from Woodstock, had been forced to recruit a new band of West Coast musicians. "It was a very tough period," he confessed to London-based disc jockey

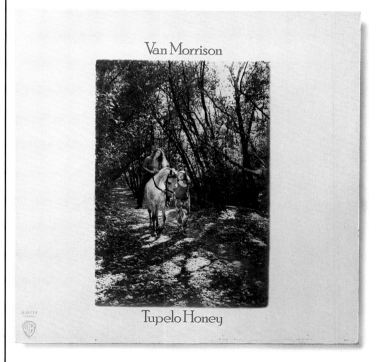

The cover of *Tupelo Honey* was shot at a friend's stable but suggested that Van and Janet had become part of the farm-owning hippy aristocracy. "An album cover is not real life," Van later complained. "An album is not real life. It's like a painting. A painting is not real life. You can't live in a painting."

In California, Van was enjoying what his wife called "a quiet life", which meant spending a lot of time at home writing music, reading and thinking or taking strolls outside. "We don't go to parties," she said. "We never go anywhere. Going on the road is the only excitement we have."

David Jensen in 1990. "I didn't want to change my band but I found myself in a position with studio time . . . and I had to ring up and get somebody in. That was the predicament I was in."

In order to promote *Tupelo Honey* effectively he needed to tour, even though he now had a phobia about performing, a strange development for the man who had made a name for himself in Belfast through his exhibitionism. He was particularly fearful of large audiences because he felt trapped by their expectations. At the Fillmore East in New York in 1971, he had angered an audience when he halted a show midway through "Cyprus Avenue" and said, "We could stop any time. We could just stop."

John Platania, who was still playing in concert with him, noticed his stage confidence ebbing away. "There were many times when he literally had to be coaxed on stage," he remembers. "His motto was 'The show does not have to go on'. He would create the choice of whether he would go on stage or not."

Years later Van explained his fears: "I've never been comfortable working live. I'm still not. I was never able to adjust to it because when I started and we played dances, you would finish a couple of songs and just walk through the audience. No stuff about being a star."

In San Francisco he played to an audience of just 200 for whom he was perfectly relaxed, and even jokingly included renditions of "Hound Dog", the Doris Day hit "Que Sera Sera" and Dylan's "Just Like a Woman". A few weeks later he was due to play at Winterland, one of the city's most prestigious venues, but two days before he announced that he was "retiring" from live performances. When he was finally persuaded to go on stage he ignored the audience throughout his set and then refused to return for an encore, until begged to by support act Taj Mahal.

For a while it looked as though he might keep his promise never to perform again, but then he discovered the Lion's Share, a small club five miles down the road in San Anselmo. He made an informal appearance with Rambling Jack Elliott, and enjoyed it so much that he began to make regular unannounced appearances. This seemed to restore his appetite for performing, because a coast-to-coast tour was set up for early 1972.

Stephen Pillster, who was later to become Van's tour manager, remembers that spontaneity was the key. "He would call up his band early in the afternoon to see if they fancied having a blow that night. I would then call the club owner who would just cut one of his acts for that night, and let the headliner open for Van. We could pretty much go in at two hours' notice."

Van's next album, *St Dominic's Preview*, is regarded as one of his best. Although not as polished as *Moondance* it was more musically adventurous than either *Street Choir* or *Tupelo Honey*. When it came out in August 1972 *Rolling Stone* greeted it as "the best-produced, most ambitious Van Morrison record yet released", and *Melody Maker* considered it "perhaps the first completely satisfying Van Morrison album since *Astral Weeks*".

Significantly it was also his first album not to have love as its major theme, for, if there was any running through *St Dominic's Preview*, it was the theme of rootlessness and the need for shelter. On it he mentions San Francisco, Belfast, Oregon, Paris and Denmark, but ultimately he's content to be a wanderer as long as he has his music.

The cover of *Tupelo Honey* had portrayed Van as a bearded, back-to-nature hippie, but for *St Dominic's Preview* he was a gypsy troubadour sitting in a doorway wearing scuffed boots, a neckerchief and a pair of unfashionable-looking jeans with an inner seam beginning to gape open.

He has since made it clear that he does not consider the covers to be significant pointers to the mood of the album inside, but there is often an unconscious link. *St Dominic's Preview* was the album of a gypsy out on the street, for whom the guitar in the hand has replaced the woman by his side.

He was obviously a musical gypsy too, still rifling that collection of records that graced the small front room of 125 Hyndford Street in his early years. There was rhythm and blues on *St Dominic's Preview*, but there was also jazz and gospel, folk and soul.

On the two longest tracks, "Listen to the Lion" and "Almost Independence Day", Van continued his experimentation with vocal sounds that began as words and then splintered into grunts, moans and

At the time of *St Dominic's Preview* Van was beginning to play more live dates, delighting in spontaneous shows in little-known clubs (*opposite*) where he could be fitted in as a last-minute addition to the bill.

yelps as he sought after a language beyond words. He pictured a lion, deep in his soul, that had to be heard, and his singing was his way of tuning in to the primal roar.

In 1973 he acquired more control over his career when he had a 16-track recording studio built alongside his home. He named it Caledonia Studios, and it was here that he recorded his next album, *Hard Nose the Highway*.

His marriage was by now in serious trouble. "When we started recording, Janet was still in the house but she was definitely on her way out," remembers John Platania. "She would make subtle complaints about the relationship but nothing specific. All that she would say was that he was difficult to live with. By the time the album was finished she had definitely left."

Divorce proceedings were set in motion and the newly hired Stephen Pillster, formerly manager of the San Francisco cult band Dan Hicks and the Hot Licks, had the job of dealing with the lawyers. It was a sad and messy business. Van was still deeply in love with Janet and wanted her to stay. He was also determined to get custody of their daughter Shana whom he adored. Janet also wanted custody in addition to half of Van's earnings for the period they were together.

George and Violet Morrison sold their house in Belfast and came to live near their son, so that they could care for Shana during this troubled time. Van bought them a small record shop, Caledonia Records, in Fairfax, California.

Hard Nose the Highway, released in July 1973, was a product of this disturbed time and reflected his shaken foundations. The albums from *Astral Weeks* onwards had been suffused with his joy of loving and being loved; now he was alone and he seemed momentarily to have been robbed of his subject-matter.

For the first time he had attempted to write social commentary with songs about the baby boom generation ("Wild Children"), and the "plastic revolutionaries" of the counter-culture ("The Great Deception"), but the style didn't suit him. Perhaps the greatest indication that he was headed for a dry period was the fact that the album contained only six Van Morrison songs. "Purple

The first half of the 1970s saw Van plunge from being a prolific and happily married artist to a divorcee with writer's block and a bad case of insecurity.

Heather" was an old song by the McPeake Family, and "Bein' Green" was taken from the children's television programme *Sesame Street*.

Writing in the music paper *Let It Rock* the British critic Charlie Gillet commented: "The trouble with *Hard Nose the Highway* is that although the music is quite often interesting, it doesn't have a convincing emotional basis. The prevailing mood is of clean country air.

"Despite the lack of lyric inspiration and of melodic focus, the record is attractive to listen to. But Van Morrison has set high standards for himself and *Hard Nose the Highway* doesn't meet them."

Van appeared quickly to forget the album, and told *Rolling Stone* in August that it was already "long gone and totally in my past. My only present is the gig tomorrow night . . . and the gig after that."

The gigs he was referring to were with the Caledonia Soul Orchestra on a nationwide tour that was attracting some of the best reviews ever of his live work. The obstinate, prickly, unpredictable performer of just two years earlier had been replaced by a confident, though virtually immobile, star. In a show that included some of the best of his material from his early Them singles through to songs from *Hard Nose the Highway*, he appeared to be scaling new heights. "I would say that that tour represented the height of his confidence as a performer," says John Platania. "Up until then it was often touch and go as to whether he'd go on stage."

The tour came to Europe and kicked off with a press conference in Amsterdam, and played six dates in England at the end of July. Two of the concerts, played at London's Rainbow Theatre on 23rd and 24th July, were recorded and later used as part of the live double album *It's Too Late to Stop Now*.

The Caledonia Soul Orchestra that consisted of Jeff Labes (keyboards), Dahaud Shaar (drums), John Platania (guitar), David Hayes (bass), Jack Shroer (sax), Bill Atwood (trumpet) and a five-piece string section was reckoned to be his best band ever. Schroer and Platania had been with him since *Moondance*.

Opposite: Van's daughter Shana accompanied him on the *Too Late to Stop Now* tour. When it reached London's Rainbow Theatre in July 1973, the two-year-old decided to join her famous father on stage.

The first real indication that Van was having problems writing was his 1973 album *Hard Nose the Highway*, which fell well below the standards set by his earlier solo albums.

Although Van was at a creative peak as a live performer he was still suffering the effects of the break-up. One new song, never recorded on an album, was called "I Paid the Price", and appeared to be about his imminent divorce.

When he returned to America there were more battles over the custody of Shana (who had accompanied him to Europe). John Platania was with him in Marin County one day when Van tried to collect her. "We went to the house where Shana was with her baby-sitter," he says. "It was a place that Van had rented for Janet after they split. He took Shana to be with him but it didn't last long. There was a big battle over that though because I don't think he was supposed to be seeing her at that time."

The divorce was finalised that year on the grounds of "irreconcilable differences". Janet took Shana to live with her and was later to remarry.

In the midst of his confusion Van surprisingly gave what were perhaps his best live shows ever with his best band, the Caledonia Soul Orchestra. Many critics reckon that few live albums in the rock genre surpass the two records that make up *Too Late to Stop Now*.

The *Too Late to Stop Now* tour is now regarded as a milestone in his performing career. After the Rainbow Theatre concerts in London, the music critic of *The Times* wrote that the ensemble playing of the Caledonia Soul Orchestra was "simply the most sophisticated and unusual I have ever heard".

CHAPTER SEVEN

A PERIOD OF TRANSITION

The break-up of his marriage in 1973 caused him to rethink his values and attitudes, sending him on a search through philosophy and religion.

THE REPERCUSSIONS OF HIS break-up with Janet had a deep effect. "He flipped," remembers John Platania. "He couldn't cope with it at all. He would cancel shows. He would talk about it as much as he possibly could, and then just go into periods of silence. But everybody knew it was killing him."

It was in the midst of this inner torment that he began to re-evaluate his life and career, and to show a renewed interest in religion. He had always had mystical inclinations but had never examined them in detail. The sense of wonder that had characterised his earlier material had diminished over the years. From folding into the mystic he had moved to hard-nosing the highway.

But the spiritual glimpses that he believed he had experienced as a child ended up as no more than tantalising nudges from beyond, and offered no words of instruction. They suggested that there was more to life than the material, but they offered no love, forgiveness or guidance.

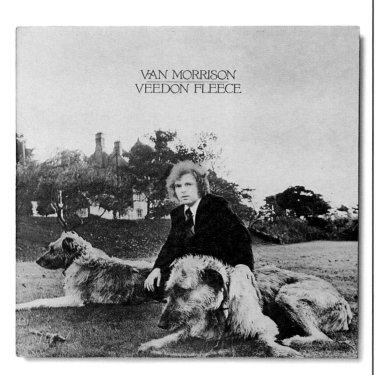

Veedon Fleece **partly drew on Van's experience of driving through Ireland on a holiday in autumn 1973. It was the beginning of his reassessment of himself as an Irish musician. The cover photo was taken in the grounds of the Sutton House Hotel.**

In times of trouble, Van could not ask his "childlike visions" for consolation. Instead he took to the bottle. By the time he moved to California he was consuming endless bottles of whisky. Janet almost succeeded in making him give up but he would then become secretive, and hide bottles in the bathroom.

"At that time there were so many strange things going on in my life," he told me in 1985. "On the one hand everything was very bright and jolly and on the other hand it was the complete opposite. So there were these contradictory things happening.

"I got the carpet pulled out from under me by a lot of people in a short space of time and that's when [my search] started. Everything was just pulled out from under me. It was over a couple of months, in 1973, when just BANG! and it was up for grabs. I had to start being responsible for me. I didn't want to be a victim of it."

An early indication of his search was a visit made to Ireland in October 1973, ostensibly to work on a documentary and to negotiate concert appearances, but actually to take a rare holiday and to get back in touch with the land he'd left six years before.

He had become interested in his Celtic origins after spending most of his life looking towards America as the source of all good music, and then realising that blues, gospel and country each owed a great debt to Scotland and Ireland.

Later, when asked what he had done during his visit, he replied: "I've relaxed and toured. I hired a car and drove to Cork, Cashel, Killarney and even saw the Blarney Stone. A lot of Irish people, even those who live here, never get to see Ireland."

The three-week visit was also significant as it stimulated him to write eight new songs, which he began recording as soon as he returned to California. They were to form the backbone of his album *Veedon Fleece*.

It was a plodding, meditative record that lacked the fire of his earlier work, and this was probably an accurate reflection of his new mood. The first side most obviously drew on the Irish visit with its mention of Irish characters, the countryside where people have "real soul" and the streets of Arklow, while the second side returned to the subject of lost love.

The Veedon Fleece, mentioned once in the song "You Don't Pull No Punches But You Don't Push the River", appears to be Van's Irish equivalent of the Holy Grail, a religious relic that would answer his questions if he could track it down on his quest around the west coast of Ireland.

Former Monarch Billy McAllen recounts the amusing story of a friend who was a Van Morrison fanatic, and who had gone to the extent of asking a professor of Irish history at Queen's University, Belfast, to trace the identity of the Veedon Fleece. "I told him that he could actually meet Van if he came round to my place one night, and then he could ask him face to face," says McAllen. "So I introduced this guy to Van but Van wasn't on good form that night. The guy got him to sign the cover of an album he had and then he said, 'By the way Van, what is the Veedon Fleece?' Van just looked at him and said, 'It doesn't mean anything. I made it up myself.' He said it as quick as that. He didn't want to elaborate."

"You Don't Pull No Punches . . . " was, he once said, inspired by what he knew about Gestalt therapy, and it contained his first reference to the poet William Blake.

Blake, who was born in London in 1757, embraced a highly unorthodox brand of Christianity that pitted Jesus Christ against God the Father. As a child he claimed to have seen angels, and in later life he fought fiercely against rationalism, believing himself to be under the direct command of higher spiritual powers. He was a popular poet in the 1960s because his anti-authoritarianism appealed to campus rebels, his ability to see "a world in a grain of sand" to acid-heads, and his belief in the innocence of children to hippies.

Stephen Pillster, Van's tour manager, saw the beginnings of this search for his Irishness when he joined him in Dublin. "I always thought Van had a tough time finding his centre," he says. "It really came to me when we were in Ireland that he's really a mad Irish poet. That's his genetic make-up.

"He's never taken particular pride in authorship. He thinks of himself more as a channel. That may be part of what sustained his quest in terms of religion and spirituality. That's where it may all have come from."

After the bohemian looks of the 1960s it was a surprise to see Van attired in a dark suit, white shirt and tie (*above*). *Veedon Fleece* contained his first mention of the English mystical poet William Blake (*right*) with whom he was beginning to identify. *Overleaf:* The Caledonia Soul Orchestra in 1974.

During 1974 Van threw himself into his work again, and it became the year of the burn-out, the year in which he realised that he had been working too hard and meditating too little. In March he returned to Dublin to play a series of concerts, but was struck down by a virus that caused him to stagger through the shows, and then forced him to cancel some English dates.

The Caledonia Soul Orchestra had a new line-up for this visit to Europe, because Van felt that in its original form it had achieved everything it possibly could and had run out of challenges. However, on its return to California, the new version was disbanded and Stephen Pillster was relieved of his duties.

When he came back to Europe later in the year to perform in Switzerland, Germany, Holland and England, Van instead chose to play with a trio of British and American session musicians, who subsequently accompanied him on a 25-date tour of America.

Following this he retreated from view. He had released seven albums since 1970, and had lived under constant pressure to write, produce, record and tour. He had reached a point where the excitement had gone and the ideas had dried up. He needed time off to build up an appetite and also to take fresh stock of himself. "I got to the point where music just wasn't doing it for me any more, a point I'd thought I would never reach," he said.

"I hadn't taken time off before and something was telling me to knock it off a bit. I caught up on years of sleep . . . When you are committed to a series of concerts you lose all the spontaneity, it's just not jazz any more. The reason I first got into music and the reason I was then doing it were conflicting. It was such a paradox."

The creative crisis was matched by a crisis of identity. Fame and attention confused him because they gave rise to personae he claimed not to recognise; these included Van the Man, Van the Mystic and the Belfast Cowboy. "There was such a conflict between being Van Morrison and being Van Morrison," he told me in 1985. "There was the Van Morrison people used to talk about in relation to what I was doing in my work sphere, and a lot of the time I wouldn't even know this person they were talking about.

With the revamped Caledonia Soul Orchestra, Van played in America and Europe along with two nights at London's Hammersmith Odeon and four nights in Dublin. The Dublin dates annoyed his fans in Northern Ireland who felt he should have given at least one show in his home city of Belfast, where he hadn't played since 1967.

"People would be sitting and talking about Van Morrison, and I'd wonder who they were talking about. I knew it wasn't me. So there was the other Van Morrison who was me and was the one I had to deal with. It was a question of putting this in perspective so that I didn't become schizophrenic.

"Being famous was extremely disappointing for me. When I became famous it was a complete drag and it still is a complete drag. It's not relevant and what people make out of it is completely unreal. It's not based on anything because the people who are saying it are not famous."

He started by stripping away the fantasies and speculations that people attached to him, and by questioning all the values that had been passed on to him. "It was then I came upon various other people who gave me pointers. I wouldn't call them 'gurus'. I would call them 'spiritual friends'. I don't believe in gurus. Sometimes somebody will say something and you go, oh, I've been thinking about that for years but nobody else has ever said it.

"So sometimes I would go on that and then I'd get off it again, and go back into the music business. You get pulled in different directions and it all depends how strong the pull is."

A secondary reason for this vigorous self-analysis was the desire to discover the meaning behind his childhood feelings of rapture. He was looking, as he said, for "somewhere to put my experiences, to find out what they were". There had been clues in the work of Blake. "That was what came close to describing what the feeling was," he said. "It still is the closest. John Donne as well. Also Yogananda [Paramhansa Yogananda, author of *Autobiography of a Yogi*], but in a different way."

He also explored what was being called the New Consciousness movement, which was a broad mix of therapies and disciplines that were united in the belief that mankind had much further to go in its evolution, and that each individual could achieve a higher potential by tapping into the life-force. He listened to tapes by Gestalt therapist Fritz Perls, began reading the *New Age Journal* and even briefly went through Transactional analysis.

"Most of these groups come to me," he explained. "If there's something in it that I can utilise for making myself better equipped to deal

Having dismissed the Caledonia Soul Orchestra Van played Britain and Europe in the summer of 1974 with session musicians Pete Wingfield (keyboards), Jermone Rimson (bass) and Dallas Taylor (drums). The tour took in festivals in Montreux, Switzerland (*above*), and Knebworth, England (*overleaf*).

with what I have to do, I want to find that and know about it and do it. But that's it. It stops there. I never join any organisation."

During this period he also suffered from writer's block. He tootled away in his home studio but wasn't happy with the results. At one point he worked with Joe Sample, the keyboard player with the Crusaders, on some studio experiments, which gave rise to speculation that he would release a Van Morrison and the Crusaders album, but nothing was released during 1975.

In May 1976 he took the unprecedented step of issuing a statement, through his record company, in order to dispel rumours that he was either retiring or about to release an album. In it he admitted that he had come to a standstill.

"I simply stopped doing it for a while in order to get a new perspective on what it was all about," he stated. "I wanted to change the way I was working. I wanted to get more of a solid business thing together. I wanted to open up new areas of creativity, so I had to let go of everything for a while. I went through a lot of personal changes. There were a lot of things within myself that I had to sort out."

At the same time he let it be known that he was planning to base his operations in Britain, "back to the roots, back to where I started".

He duly arrived back in London, persuaded top promoter Harvey Goldsmith to become his manager, and set about a return to recording at the Manor Studios in Shipton-on-Cherwell, Oxfordshire, with Mac Rebennack (Dr John) as his keyboard player and co-producer.

Recording progressed slowly as Van abandoned various experiments and released different musicians, until he came up with what he considered to be the right line-up. At one time he even tried a track with Chris Barber's jazz band.

In the period between overdubbing the album in Los Angeles and its release in 1977, Van agreed to appear at The Band's farewell performance in San Francisco, alongside contemporaries such as Bob Dylan, Eric Clapton and Neil Young. It was to be an extravagant affair that would be recorded for a triple album, and filmed for cinema release by director Martin Scorsese.

A Period of Transition (1977) was a comeback album loaded with expectations, but it didn't live up to them. Van's chief collaborator on the project was New Orleans musician Mac Rebennack, better known to rock fans as Dr John "the Night Tripper".

The collaboration between Dr John and Van happened at a time when he was feeling the pull back to England. He had just engaged the services of London promoter Harvey Goldsmith as his manager.

On Thanksgiving Day, November 1976, Van took part in The Band's farewell concert which was filmed by Martin Scorsese for the feature-length documentary *The Last Waltz*. He is pictured with Bob Dylan (centre) and Band member Robbie Robertson. It was Robertson who supplied Van with the nickname the Belfast Cowboy – meaning that he was really an American who had accidentally been born in Northern Ireland.

He became terribly nervous half an hour before he was due on stage, and rushed back to his hotel to change his clothes. Harvey Goldsmith had to coax him back to the venue, where he went on to join Richard Manuel of The Band in "Tura Lura Lural". He also delivered an impressive performance of "Caravan", which gave a boost to his career when the movie, *The Last Waltz*, was released.

There was great anticipation amongst the music critics for the new record, *A Period of Transition*, on its eventual release in April 1977, because it was assumed that Van would have a lot to deliver after his two-and-a-half-year absence from the studio. Yet despite its promising title the album was lethargic and uninspired except for "Joyous Sound", an optimistic track with a tinge of gospel, which offered the only clue to his future direction and was released as a single.

Yet perhaps it was the album he needed to make to rid himself of the clutter surrounding his brain, and to deal with the intimidating wave of expectation surrounding his career. As he said in June 1977, "I think I needed to break a lot of that expectancy down. I know from experience that I go to see some artists expecting a particular thing. If they don't come up with that then I'm disappointed, but if I have no expectations they usually do something I haven't heard before and I'm turned on. The moment you expect something, you never get it."

Surprisingly, he agreed to support the record by doing press and radio interviews, although he clearly found it a tiresome exercise. The unco-operative characteristics that had been noted in him from childhood were displayed for all to see.

In a notorious live interview on Capital Radio with disc jockey Nicky Horne, he was so taciturn that Horne was forced continually to play music in order to disguise his hostility. When asked why he wanted to do interviews after such a long period of silence, he replied: "I don't want to do anything . . . What I'm doing right now is I'm doing an interview for promotional purposes, no more and no less than that. There's an album, so I'm available for talking."

Although *A Period of Transition* wasn't the album his fans had hoped for, it was the album he had to make to get his creative juices working again. He admits to working at his best when expectations of his product are at their lowest.

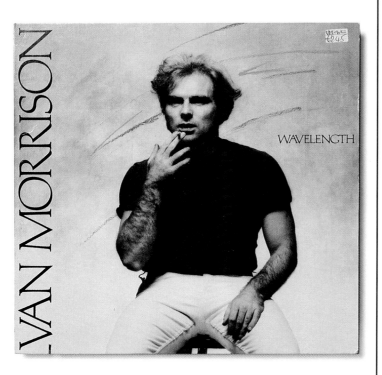

It was with *Wavelength* that he really came bounding back. The cover showed a fitter, more relaxed Van who was willing to promote himself. The music inside was likewise leaner and more accessible.

In an ideal world Van Morrison would write songs and then play them, at a time and place of his choosing of course, to a few hundred people. The making and promoting of records, the necessary packaging of the music as a product, and the need to pass information to the public irritated him.

His next album, *Wavelength*, was also recorded at the Manor, and featured his old friend from Belfast Herbie Armstrong on guitar, former member of Them Peter Bardens on keyboards, Peter Van Hooke on drums and Mickey Feat on bass guitar.

This time he returned with a confident, rocky collection that was guaranteed to receive airplay. The cover photograph, by Norman Seeff, was an attractive black and white portrait of Van in new casual clothes and, for the first time, he had a smile on his face.

The title track was both a reference to his habit as a child of tuning in to the Voice of America on his radio, and also a love song. "Kingdom Hall" is a playful consideration of the power of music. In "Checkin' It Out" he addresses his lover and tells her that whatever problems they may have, there are "guides and spirits all along the way", an indication of his New Age explorations. "I'm working with concepts which aren't concerned with the top twenty or how I look," he said. "They're not related to the modern world. In fact many of my concepts relate to people who aren't around any more. It's a matter of trying to find your space in this, trying to find your shape."

In September 1978 he began his first major tour in four years, a ten-week tour of America with the band who had played on *Wavelength*. It began in San Francisco and moved through major cities including Los Angeles, New York, Washington and Chicago.

At the end of the tour, it was announced that he would be playing an extensive tour of Britain and Ireland, which would include two concerts in Belfast, the first time he had played in his home city in twelve years.

For the fans in Belfast it was a memorable occasion. The most famous and influential musician from Northern Ireland was back home and playing. Van took the opportunity of revisiting Cyprus Avenue and Sandy Row with a film crew again in tow, but when questioned about the significance of the event he played it down. "I don't feel one way or the other," he said. "I don't feel emotional or unemotional. I just feel I'm doing the job. My job is to play music and deliver the show. That's what I do. It's more emotional for the audience I think . . . what they sort of think you are."

Radio played a great rôle in Van's early musical education, and in his memories of the "days before rock'n'roll", the "wireless" frequently makes an appearance.

Chapter Eight

Into the Music

The *Wavelength* album proved to be the start of a new era in which Van again began performing with confidence and making commercially successful records.

After the 1978 tour Van returned to California to begin recording *Into the Music*, again with Herbie Armstrong on guitar and Peter Van Hooke on drums, but this time he brought in Mark Jordan on keyboards, David Hayes on bass, Pee Wee Ellis on saxophone, Marc Isham on trumpet and Toni Marcus on violin and mandolin.

Most of the songs had been written while Van was staying with Herbie Armstrong in the village of Epwell, in Oxfordshire. "Rolling Hills" was written about the Cotswold countryside which he spent much of his time exploring by car. Sometimes he would take his guitar with him and walk through fields making up songs, just as Wordsworth used to compose out loud while walking through the woods.

"The songwriter Kenny Young lived about four miles from my house," remembers Armstrong. "One day he was taking a short cut down a tiny lane and he saw this guy in a field with his guitar. He couldn't believe his eyes. He pulled up his car to take a closer look and it was Van!"

Into the Music **was Van's most consciously spiritual album to date, with tinges of gospel and a celebration of the forces of nature. Mostly written in the Cotswold countryside of England it was an indication of albums to come.**

Into the Music was an optimistic album that appeared to celebrate a rejuvenation of his love life, as well as a rekindling of his appetite for things spiritual. The theme of renewal and healing now appeared almost Christian. In "Full Force Gale" he was lifted up by "the Lord", and gave an impression of delivery from destruction by sudden conversion. In "Rolling Hills" he portrayed himself reading the Bible and living a life "in Him".

The album gave rise to speculation of a "born-again" Van Morrison. After all, his friend Bob Dylan was now writing fiery gospel songs that would make their début on his album *Slow Train Coming*, and had been spotted studying the New Testament at a Bible school in Los Angeles.

But whereas Dylan's new songs were evangelistic and drew on specific sections of the Bible, Van's were closer to nature mysticism than to gospel. In both songs that specifically mention "the Lord", it is in the setting of nature.

I asked Van whether it was fair to describe him as a nature mystic. "To a degree," he said, "but it's not the whole picture. I would say that I'm a Christian mystic."

Why Christian? "Well, because I'm not a Buddhist or a Hindu. I'm a Christian. I was born in a Christian environment in a Christian country, and I was born after the Christ event, so that makes me a Christian."

Was his image of God personal or impersonal? "It's both." Did the God he believed in have feelings about Van Morrison? "It would be very hard for me to say right now. At this point in time it would be very difficult to say. I'd prefer not to answer that question really."

When asked about the theme of rebirth which has appeared consistently throughout his work, he said: "I wrote a song called 'Full Force Gale' in which I said 'No matter where I roam/I will find my way back home/I will always return to the Lord'. That answers it for me. No matter what I might say at the present, that's my feeling about that.

"Sometimes I fluctuate. When you say to me 'Christian', that's got about twenty lights going off."

What kept him searching? "It's not that I'm searching. It's like I'm receiving guidance to do

this. I'm not searching. I'm receiving some sort of inner direction. There is something inside me which directs me to do this, and I don't know why yet myself."

Did this "something inside" direct him to do his work? "To do my work and my study. To study religion and to study various aspects of this in relation to experiences."

If evidence was needed that he had not become a born-again Christian, it was provided on his next album, *Common One*, which was recorded in the south of France in February 1980. It demonstrated that he had an appetite for the whole New Age smorgasbord, from earth energy and Arthurian legend to Blakeian reverie and Yeatsian trance-states.

This was his most self-indulgent album to date. Each track was like a separate prayer or meditation, and it seemed as if he had hoped the truth would reveal itself to him as he dived deep into his sub-consciousness, and dredged up its residue of images.

In "Summertime in England" he tipped the balance from inspired improvisation to embarrassing ramble. Here, instead of walking in the steps of Blake and Eliot in order to see what insights their approach to art would provide today, he merely mentioned them by name, as though it would be enough to impress his audience that he read serious literature. "Did you ever hear about Wordsworth and Coleridge baby?" must be one of his least inspired lines.

For his next album, *Beautiful Vision*, he tightened up the lyrics, although the quest for meaning remained the same. Around this time he was dating a Danish girl, Ulla Munch, who came from the Vanlose district of Copenhagen, which explains the title "Vanlose Stairway", and could be the key to the instrumental "Scandinavia" and other songs where a woman is presented as a saviour-figure.

In "She Gives Me Religion" he mentions walking back down "mystic avenue", an obvious reference to his experience of Cyprus Avenue. He hears the church bells (of St Donard's) and the "angel of imagination" opens up his gaze.

The whole album is in one way or another concerned with the nature of what he refers to in

Common One, recorded in the South of France, was less accessible than its predecessor and showed Van's growing interest in New Age teachings. *Opposite:* Performing during his 1979 British tour.

VAN MORRISON
BEAUTIFUL VISION

By the time of *Beautiful Vision*, Van had switched his base back to London where he was photographed (*opposite*) in a West End restaurant. He bought a house in Holland Park, close to the Notting Hill area – where he had lived during his days with Them – and to Ladbroke Grove which was mentioned in "Slim Slow Slider" on *Astral Weeks*.

"Beautiful Vision" as his "mystical rapture". He captures his vision most clearly in "Dweller on the Threshold" and "Across the Bridge Where Angels Dwell", in which he describes a world in which the heavenly realm is just beyond what we can hear and see, rather than baldly stating "I am in ecstasy", as he had done in "Beautiful Vision".

Van had by now finally made the move back to England. After alternating between California and a home in Oxfordshire, he returned to his old stamping-ground of west London, where he bought a small house in Holland Park.

Over the next decade he was to become a familiar figure around Holland Park and Notting Hill; he would take snatched lunches in local patisseries and small cafés, saunter along Holland Park Avenue with such neighbours as Elvis Costello and Shane MacGowan of the Pogues, or stroll in the park itself.

During the late seventies and early eighties he had been managed by Bill Graham Management of San Francisco. Now that he was in London he employed Belfast-born Paul Charles to handle "business arrangements", as the sleeve of *Beautiful Vision* delicately put it.

Charles saw his job as being to place Van firmly back in the public consciousness. "I think it was during this period that he did the groundwork for what he is today," says Charles. "It was important that people didn't just see him as the mystic from the late sixties and early seventies.

"There were things that Van would do and things he wouldn't [to promote himself], and the idea was to make the touring very very effective.

"Most acts have visibility and sell lots of albums by having hit singles. People like Van don't have hit singles and so you have to find another tool, and in his case the other tool was touring. We had to make the tours his hit singles.

"That's why we'd go into the Dominion Theatre in Tottenham Court Road and do eleven nights. It would be an event. If he had done one night in Hammersmith it would have been all over too soon. He always put on great, great concerts. He proved that he is one of the best singers around."

Beautiful Vision was launched in March 1983 with a four-night run at the Dominion, which

Van Morrison.

restored any doubts that might have arisen over previous lacklustre performances. During sets that often lasted more than ninety minutes, he delivered some blistering soul that was received with gratitude by the critics.

At this time he gave a significant interview to Dermot Stokes of the Dublin music paper *Hot Press*, in which he spoke of his research into music as a healing force. "I've done some research," he said, "into ancient teachings about the effect of different keys. Apparently if someone was sick they used to get a harp and play a C chord, or whatever, to heal the affliction. These teachings are still floating around in various sects. They've been lost but you can still dig them out."

His research was now leading him to speculate that "intensity experiences" could be initiated by certain forms of music. He remembered that his first inexplicable feeling of wonder had been at 125 Hyndford Street, while he was listening to the voice of Mahalia Jackson (mentioned in "Summertime in England" as a voice coming "through the ether"). Was it possible to create music that stimulated beautiful visions and mystical raptures?

As he read books like Cyril Scott's *Music: Its Secret Influence through the Ages* (1937), he began to understand that he had always viewed music as a transforming power, but had found himself in an industry in which gross receipts were the measure of success. "I knew what I was doing in music back in 1966 or 1967," he told me, "but I was trying to translate this into having a band and selling albums. I was in the wrong framework. I was trying to do meditation at the Fillmore East, if you know what I mean! In fact, I can remember being on stage there and thinking, I'm in the wrong place at the wrong time. I knew what I was doing with my music but there was no channel to put it across. It wasn't 'rock'n'roll', it wasn't 'get it on', it wasn't 'boogie'."

He explained that the effect he wanted his music to have was "ideally to induce states of meditation and ecstasy, as well as to make people think", and said that he considered this effect to be a "spiritual experience".

At the same time he was becoming interested in the Church of Scientology, possibly after friends like Robin Williamson (formerly of the Incredible

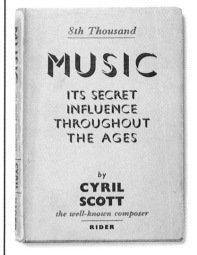

In 1983 he revealed his interest in the power of music to alter consciousness. One of the books he was reading at the time was Cyril Scott's *Music: Its Secret Influence Throughout the Ages*.

String Band) and Nicky Hopkins (keyboard player on many Rolling Stones albums) had enthused about their involvement. He was in contact with the Church of Scientology in London and San Francisco, read founder L. Ron Hubbard's handbook *Dianetics: The Modern Science of Mental Health*, and then embarked on a course of counselling, or "auditing" as it is referred to.

In May 1983 Gavin Martin reported in the *New Musical Express* that "Van has now reached such a stage in the heightening of his consciousness that he's now a counsellor for the sect. Each night before he plays to packed houses in the nearby Dominion Theatre, he can be found walking about the centre, giving advice or reading from the works of the mighty Mr Hubbard."

Van has since denied that he has ever been a counsellor, and this is confirmed by the Church's British headquarters in East Grinstead, who say that he had sessions at home with a freelance auditor, who would have worked with him to "eradicate various negative aspects", and to move him towards a state of mind that is known as a "clear".

"Van wouldn't be someone who we would term a Scientologist," said an auditor. "I think he liked what he had but he wasn't that smitten that he wanted to do it full time. He only came down to East Grinstead once, and I think he eventually finished what we call fourth grade, which is about three-quarters of the way to being a clear."

At this level he should apparently have been "happy with his ability to communicate, be unworried by upsets and able to take up new ventures without any trouble".

Did the new Van emerge? "I know he didn't like performing too much, and I think to some degree whatever was behind that got handled. He was happier about being on stage after that. I know he started doing more live concerts and having hit albums. Obviously there were improvements and changes."

The album *Inarticulate Speech of the Heart* (1983) alerted Van's audience to his new involvement, for included among the credits was a note of "special thanks" to L. Ron Hubbard. However, when questioned about Scientology he has always

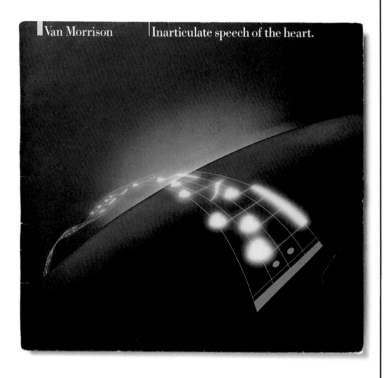

In the sleeve notes to *Inarticulate Speech of the Heart*, Van offered "special thanks" to L. Ron Hubbard, the creator of Scientology. It led to speculation that he had become a fully-fledged Scientologist and even that he was working as a counsellor for the organisation.

remained far from expansive, admitting that he "did some levels" but denying that he has ever been into the movement. "It was when I started to get into the organisation that I didn't want to do it any more," he said. "I hate organisations and I think there are a lot of people in the organisation who haven't got a clue."

Inarticulate Speech of the Heart was a move towards creating music for meditation; it contained a lot of synthesiser sounds from Mark Isham, and some uilleann pipes and low flute from Davy Spillane. Four out of the eleven tracks were instrumental, and when there were lyrics they were sparse and repetitive, more like chants than fully developed narratives.

If there was a theme uniting the various songs it was the theme of homecoming, of returning to his roots. "Connswater" and "Celtic Swing" were evocations of the sound of Ireland, and "Irish Heartbeat" was a promise to return to his "own ones".

When asked by Bill Flanagan of *Musician* magazine what kept him moving, he answered: "It's just an internal thing. It's like getting back to your roots. You live in a lot of different places and it gives you a broader perspective on life in general. One becomes very cosmopolitan. But there's a big part of me that's just strictly involved with the island of Ireland." In the same interview he commented that "Celtic Ray", from *Common One*, with its image of the mothers of England, Scotland, Ireland and Wales calling their children back, was a "Celtic invocation. There's nothing political about it."

The search for meaning now dominated his songwriting, and rendered his new material almost inaccessible to anyone who was not a fellow seeker. Earlier in his career he had combined more ordinary observations with his religious insights, but on *A Sense of Wonder* (1984) every Morrison track was a digression that spoke of non-specific shiny lights and fiery visions.

In the song "A New Kind of Man", Van promoted the belief that we were entering a new stage of evolution. "I named it after a book on William Blake," Van said. "The book stresses the point that Blake was very New Age and that maybe

By 1984 it was clear that as a songwriter Van was preoccupied with matters of the spirit rather than the flesh, even though he was reportedly in love with a Danish girl, Ulla Munch, who was regularly accompanying him on tours.

He boldly claimed to have No Guru, No Method, No Teacher, yet was still most interested in gurus, methods and teachers. The Secret Heart of Music was a weekend conference which he helped organise to discuss ways in which human consciousness could be altered through music.

this could develop now. I think it's a possibility but I think it would be very difficult, because at the present time you have your Future Shock, and it's very difficult to deal with that and have your New Age at the same time."

Van paid a visit to a "church" in Hampshire, where an American Indian by the name of White Eagle was revered as a "realised master". He met the director of the Alaister Hardy Research Centre (formerly the Religious Experience Research Centre) in Oxford, and then made contact with the Wrekin Trust, an organisation that had been set up in 1971 by Sir George Trevelyan "to awaken the vision of the spiritual nature of man and the universe, and to help people to develop themselves as vehicles for channelling spiritual energies into society".

The Wrekin Trust was of particular interest to Van because one of its directors, Malcolm Lazarus, had organised conferences with names like "The Power of Music to Change Consciousness", and "Music, Mathematics and Consciousness".

"I think it was in 1985 that Mick Brown, a writer from the *Sunday Times*, got in touch with me and said that Van was looking for a spiritual dimension for his music," recalls Lazarus. "I was doing a conference in Winchester and Van came down, and although he found it a bit heavy-going he· got something out of it. He then decided he wanted to do something of his own."

During 1986 he released *No Guru, No Method, No Teacher*, the title being a response to those who wondered whose disciple he was. The song from which the line was taken, "In the Garden", looks back at the young Van in Hyndford Street. The mentions of "childlike vision" and going "into a trance" allude to "Madame George".

The album's opening track, "Got to Go Back", states a theme that was to be repeated over the next few years, that of having been "lifted up" as a child, and of the need to "go back" to that time in order to be healed.

The following year Van set about organising his own conference under the auspices of the Wrekin Trust. It was titled "The Secret Heart of Music" ("an exploration into the power of music to change consciousness"), and took place in September at

Loughborough University. It included lectures on "Music, Magic and Mysticism", "The Effect of Music on Hormonal Secretions in the Endocrine Glands" and "Music as a Force in Spiritual Development". There were also performances by Van, Robin Williamson, Nishat Khan, Derek Bell of the Chieftains and Anthony Rooley with the Consort of Musicke. The aim of the conference, according to the brochure, was to "help restore music to a central place in our culture as a unifying and transcendent force".

The biographical notes in the brochure revealed the way in which Van now viewed himself: "His passion for music and his bemusement with the contradictions inherent in being famous have led him to deeply question many of the underlying attitudes of our age.

"In particular, he has investigated the esoteric influences on music with a view to discovering more about its effect on the body-mind relationship. His own work is now increasingly intended as a means for inducing contemplation and for healing and uplifting the soul . . .

"His struggle to reconcile the mythic, almost otherworldly vision of the Celts, and his own search for spiritual satisfaction, with the apparent hedonism of blues and soul music has produced many inspired and visionary performances."

Malcolm Lazarus, who organised workshops in which people underwent consciousness-raising through music, remains puzzled by Van's obvious desire to learn more about the effects of music on consciousness, yet apparent unwillingness to undergo any sessions himself. "He knew there was something valuable there," says Lazarus. "He was engaged in a sort of battle between not being able to grasp the intellectual dynamics and nevertheless wanting to, and between not being willing to grasp the experiential side and yet, at the same time, wanting to incorporate it into his music.

"I think that, like a lot of artists, he was afraid to do anything to the creative process. It's a reasonable fear. It's like, what would I do without my neuroses?"

During this period Van wrote and recorded *Poetic Champions Compose*, in which he confused his heavenly and earthly loves to the extent that it was

During The Secret Heart of Music, Van performed a show for which he paid for musicians to be flown over from New York.

difficult to tell whether he was singing about God, his woman or a woman who had led him to God.

"Give Me My Rapture", a song that was definitely addressed to God, was the most blatant expression of his spiritual search. In it he beseeched the Almighty to fill him with "wonder" and to give him his "rapture today". In the same song he could appear to be singing as an orthodox Christian, as it contains traces of the Psalms in its words and thoughts, and also of Celtic hymnody. But, as Bill Flanagan, editor of *Musician* magazine, noted, Van rarely displays any sense of penitence, or any acknowledgement that God may demand something from him in return for His blessings.

Chris Hodgkin, a former personal assistant who worked with him in setting up "The Secret Heart of Music", remembers that he seemed to be mainly interested in theosophy and mystical tradition. "He tended to align himself with Christianity," recalls Hodgkin, "but he was also into pre-Christian things. I would say that he was more interested in the Western mystical tradition. He was a pretty weird Christian."

Poetic Champions Compose was the album Van was writing during the time of The Secret Heart of Music. *Opposite:* On stage at the Ulster Hall, Belfast, 1985.

CHAPTER NINE

TAKE ME WAY WAY BACK

The predominant theme of his albums over the last five years has been a longing to return to his childhood days in Belfast.
Left: **During a surprise performance at the Errigle Inn, Belfast, in 1990.**

THE SUCCESS OF "The Secret Heart of Music" prompted Van to consider disseminating his ideas in ways other than songwriting. He was constantly frustrated by the limitations of his chosen medium, and toyed with the idea of setting up a centre that would combine his office with a space where people could investigate ways of combining New Age ideas with music.

Journalist Mick Brown, who had introduced Van to the Wrekin Trust, recalls him being excited by the idea of bringing together like-minded people, to explore the matters of spirituality and consciousness-raising. "He wanted to do something more than music, and he was talking about having a small group or organisation that would put out a newsletter," he recalls. "Then he would wonder whether he should be giving lectures, or whether he should be giving lectures that included music. He wanted somehow to get involved in some kind of 'networking' activity."

In February 1988, with the idea of setting up a centre, Van moved his offices from London to Bath, in Avon. Bath had always appealed to him. It had been one of the first English towns to respond to Them in a big way, and its quiet, ancient streets appealed to his need for calm. It was close to Glastonbury, legendary burial place of the Celtic King Arthur, and also to Woolhall Studios, where he had recently been recording.

Although there had been a consistent Irish feel to his albums, it was only when Van performed with the Chieftains on a television special for St Patrick's Day in March 1988 that he made "explicit what had long been implicit in his music", as Bill Graham put it in *Hot Press*.

He had been aware of the Chieftains since his teenage days (the group had formed in 1963), and had played with them at the Edinburgh Festival during the late seventies.

The show was such a success that together they set up a tour, which began on 30th April in Aberdeen and wended its way down to London in mid-May.

The critical response was almost ecstatic. London's *Evening Standard* was the most restrained, and called the collaboration "a marriage of convenience which worked". Far more typical were the *New Musical Express*, which called it "awesome", and *Melody Maker*: "You left, at the last, transformed . . . You have just watched genius culminate, pass the utmost. A wondrous sight." All the reviews stated that for the first time Van Morrison seemed to be enjoying himself on stage. He was looking relaxed, cracking jokes and laughing.

His collaboration with the Chieftains in 1988 was widely viewed as a "marriage made in heaven". It enabled Van to enjoy himself more on stage and was an appropriate vehicle through which to explore his Irish roots.

The successful experiment led naturally to an album, *Irish Heartbeat*, on which Van and the Chieftains interpreted seven traditional Irish songs (from both sides of the border), one Scottish song and two previously recorded Morrison songs ("Celtic Ray" from *Beautiful Vision*, and "Irish Heartbeat" from *Inarticulate Speech of the Heart*).

Once again most critics were united in their praise. *New Musical Express* thought the album recaptured "the exuberance and intensity of those historic shows, thus preserving some of the most fervent performances of Morrison's career so far". *Rolling Stone* awarded it four stars and praised its "splendour and intense beauty".

Ironically it was the *Belfast Telegraph* that found it only "good in parts", and complained that if Van was to sing his version of "My Langan Love" at a party in Belfast, "people would leave early", and that if Patrick Kavanagh had lived to hear his interpretation of "Raglan Road", there'd be "trouble in the Dublin pubs". The message from the *Belfast Telegraph* seemed to be that Van was not authentic enough; he was a dabbler.

Yet despite the levity on stage and the overall feeling of celebration on *Irish Heartbeat*, Van himself was no more happy to be promoting his product. The interviews that were conducted during an all-day session at Kensington's Tara Hotel, in the company of Chieftain Paddy Moloney, all bore a striking similarity, mainly owing to Van's delivering the same grumpy answers to the same questions.

Liam Mackey of Ireland's *Hot Press* was given a particularly gruelling time as Van feigned boredom, challenged his line of questioning and accused him of dirt-digging. Van's position, as ever, was that there was nothing to explain. How did he meet up with the Chieftains? "It doesn't really matter who contacted who." How did their personalities gel? "It's got nothing to do with personalities." Why did he choose the Chieftains? "That's a stupid question really." Why did they choose those particular songs to record? "There is no why. You just do something because at the time that's the thing to do."

His conclusion, and one that he has repeated in different ways over the years, was that there was no secret to be discovered about his way of working. Making music was just his job. No one interviewed

New Musical Express thought that *Irish Heartbeat* preserved "some of the most fervent performances of Morrison's career so far". Left to right: Kevin Conneff (bodhran), Matt Molloy (flute), Paddy Moloney (uileann pipes, tin whistles), Van Morrison, Sean Keane (fiddle), Martin Fay (fiddle, bones) and Derek Bell (harp, tiompan, keyboards).

plumbers about each job they completed. "Generally, people read too much into what I do. There's nothing to read into it at all. There is no mystery. What I do is very simple. My songs, my music, my whole schtick is not something that is mysterious."

In the summer of 1988 his daughter Shana, who was still living with her mother in California, came to London to visit him. She was now a tall, beautiful seventeen-year-old who towered above her father and was often mistaken for his new girlfriend when she accompanied him to gigs.

Despite the rupture of his marriage when Shana was still a baby, he had grown close to her and had seen a lot of her during his extended stays in Mill Valley, where he still kept a home. She was now learning classical piano and having her voice trained. Sometimes they would make music together, father on sax and daughter on keyboards. "She's going through her teenage years and I'm going through mid-life crisis," he commented to writer Stephen Davis. "It matches up. We're running parallel!"

In October Van played at the Royal Albert Hall with the Chieftains, and this time he was apparently glaring rather than gleaming, and not quite at his ecstatic best. *Melody Maker* reported: "When he is not in touch with the muse that drives him, when, in concert especially, he can't find his rhythm and seems to be closed in by the humdrum, Morrison has often down the years been inclined to give up, retreat behind unconvincing façades of competence, routine readings of his devotional hymns."

In *Avalon Sunset*, which was released in May 1989, Van returned to the familiar themes of the past decade: God, woman, his childhood in Belfast and those enchanted moments when time stands still. As always, the woman, whether real or imaginary, is portrayed in religious terms ("Contacting My Angel"), and God is seen in sexual terms ("When Will I Ever Learn to Live in God"); and on a track like "Coney Island" we are offered God, sex, Ulster and timeless moments all in one song.

Again he appeared to be making specifically Christian indications. On "Whenever God Shines His Light", for which he purposely chose the well-known evangelical Cliff Richard to accompany him, he sings, "He heals the sick and heals the lame/Says

Top: **Backstage at the Hammersmith Odeon, London, with Screaming Lord Sutch (in top hat), Queen guitarist Brian May (second from right) and Moody Blues bass player John Lodge.** *Bottom:* **With jazz pianist Mose Allison, 1990.**

you can do it too in Jesus' name", and "When Will I Ever Learn to Live in God" is the closest he had ever come to true penitence.

Yet in calling the album *Avalon Sunset* he was obviously still drawing on Celtic mythology, and when asked by Gavin Martin of *New Musical Express* about the state of his spiritual search, he answered: "I'm into all of it, orthodox or otherwise. I don't accept or reject any of it. I'm not searching for anything in particular. I'm just groping in the dark . . . for a bit more light. That's it really."

He felt under constant pressure to re-examine Christianity, not just because its teachings surrounded him in childhood, but because he so often met people in the music business who were Christians, and who were only too keen to tell him that they had already received what he was looking for.

Herbie Armstrong, his old friend from Belfast, had been suddenly converted in 1988 through a pentecostal church in Notting Hill Gate. He conveyed his new-found enthusiasm to Van, who was taken aback that his hedonistic friend should be attempting to persuade him to become a convert. "I now play music for pure love and love of every day, and it's definitely through Jesus Christ and the Church that I've come back," Herbie told the *Van Morrison Newsletter* in 1990. "He's put something back into me and I'm praying that perhaps one day Van will find the Lord, because Van is checking it out and he certainly knew about the Lord long before I did."

Another friend from Belfast, Bill Dunn, had become the pastor of an Elim church, and met up with Van shortly after *Avalon Sunset* was released. "We talked for a long time about the old days," Dunn told the *Belfast Telegraph*. "A lot of what we said is confidential, but I'm still glad to say Van is my friend. Perhaps one day he will find the light just as I have done."

Many people assumed, because of the religious nature of his songs, that Van had been a "born-again" Christian for years. The duet with Cliff Richard, which saw Van enter the top ten for the first time since "Here Comes the Night" in 1965, appeared to confirm this. He began to receive invitations to play in churches and to take part in Christian arts festivals.

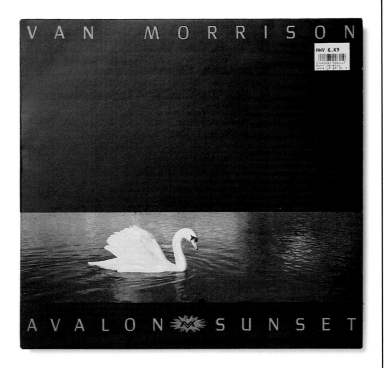

HMV 6.49

Avalon Sunset was his first UK album for Polydor after a decade with Mercury. It provided "Whenever God Shines His Light", the only British top-twenty single of his solo career, which he recorded with England's most consistent hit-maker Cliff Richard. *Opposite:* In concert at London's Finsbury Park, June 1990.

For a while he contemplated making a tour of British churches, not for evangelistic reasons, but because he felt the mood and setting of a church would be conducive to the sort of spiritual experience he was hoping to provide with his music. The tour did not materialise but he did play a one-off concert at St Mary's Church in Stogumber, Somerset, in January 1990. It was attended by a sell-out crowd of 300 as he would only agree to make the appearance if it was kept small and informal. The concert raised around £3,000, which was used to renovate a unique nineteenth-century wall painting in the church.

Following closely behind *The Best of Van Morrison* in 1990 came *Enlightenment*, which mined the same terrain as *Avalon Sunset*; it contained a Blakeian song ("Youth of 1,000 Summers"), a Belfast in the 1950s song ("In the Days Before Rock'n'Roll"), an I-need-your-help-baby song ("See Me Through"), and a rebirth song ("Start All Over Again").

After touring extensively towards the end of the year, with Andy Fairweather Low (formerly of Amen Corner) and Georgie Fame as his support acts, Van sold his home in Holland Park and moved to a house in Little Somerford, in Wiltshire. In Belfast his father, George Morrison, died suddenly of a heart attack. He was 68.

In March 1991 two documentary projects in which he had been involved were screened within days of each other. The first, "One Irish Rover", was a portrait for the BBC series *Arena*, and the second, "Coney Island of the Mind", was part of a Channel 4 series called *Without Walls*, and specifically examined the relationship between Van's work and contemporary Irish poetry.

"Coney Island of the Mind" was, at Van's suggestion, an exercise in discovering the relationship between poetry, music and mysticism. It involved him in discussions with Irish poets Michael Longley, Seamus Deane and John Montague, and visits to Cyprus Avenue and Orangefield School.

"I started to write songs at a very early age," he said. "I didn't have a clue what I was doing. Later on I was trying to find a way to connect what I was doing with my contemporaries.

By 1990, when *Enlightenment* was released, he was working regularly with keyboard player Georgie Fame who he had first met in London with the Monarchs. In January of that year he played a surprise concert at St Mary's Church, Stogumber, Somerset (*opposite*) after being approached by a local schoolteacher.

The 1990s have seen Van taking part in a never-ending tour, playing everything from major rock venues and outdoor festivals to Irish inns and Welsh pubs. He says that the playing of the music is all that counts. All the rest is a distraction.

"I discovered, however, that I was writing what some people call transcendental poetry. Other people call it mysticism in poetry. Other people call it nature poetry. Why was I writing this kind of poetry when my contemporaries weren't?

"I wanted to find out where I stood and what tradition I came from. Well, eventually, I found that the tradition I belong to is actually my own tradition. It was like getting hit over the head with a baseball bat."

For "One Irish Rover" he was filmed on the Hill of the Muses in Athens, playing "Crazy Love" with Bob Dylan and then with his band, and playing with John Lee Hooker.

In the same month Tom Jones released an album, *Carrying a Torch*, for which Van had written and produced four songs. Van had pursued Jones: "He said he had this one song 'Carrying a Torch' that he had recorded, but when he played it back he thought, Tom Jones," Jones later explained. The song was to become the album's title track, and also one of 21 songs on Van's new double album *Hymns to the Silence*.

In the songs "Professional Jealousy" and "Why Must I Always Explain?", he complained about the hardships of being a respected songwriter. The irony of "Why Must I Always Explain?" was that the thrust of his songwriting had always been explanation, giving his public detailed information about his problems, hardships and spiritual adventures. He had dropped hints about which authors he was reading and what he was listening to, and then appeared to be taken aback that his fans should ask for more.

"On Hyndford Street" referred back in both style and content to "In the Days Before Rock'n'Roll" and "Coney Island", but now specifically interpreted the warm feelings of his childhood and music as being religious: "Feeling wondrous and lit up inside/With a sense of everlasting life".

It was really *Astral Weeks* all over again, but whereas *Astral Weeks* was a series of impressions injected with religious images, his subsequent musings on the same subject had become much more explicit: footnotes to the original poem.

In "See Me Through Part II" and "Take Me Back" he explored the same subject. He wanted to

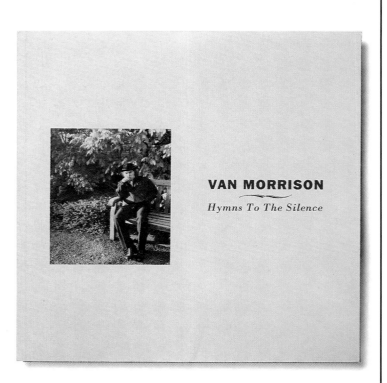

VAN MORRISON

Hymns To The Silence

On *Hymns to the Silence* his nostalgia for the Belfast of his childhood and the search for religious significance reached a crescendo in which the two themes became inextricably entwined. Although stretched over a double album, the music never wavered. The cover photograph was taken in Holland Park, close to his London home.

In March 1991 Van wrote and produced four tracks for Tom Jones, who was trying to lay his Las Vegas image to rest and resurrect himself as a man with roots in soul and rhythm and blues. The same month Van was seen in a BBC documentary "One Irish Rover", for which it was arranged for him to sing "Crazy Love" with Bob Dylan on the Hill of the Muses in Athens (*overleaf*).

VAN MORRISON'S birthplace in Hyndford Street, East Belfast was put on the map this week. American blues star Buddy Guy did the honours by unveiling a plaque to commemorate Van's roots. A "Private Eye" cartoonist, left, gives an alternative view of the event.

Some forms of recognition Van accepts and some he rejects. When Belfast blues fan Rob Braniff (*above*, right) chose to have a plaque put up at 125 Hyndford Street, Van considered it an "invasion of privacy" and tried to have it stopped. Six months later when he was offered an honorary doctorate of letters by the University of Ulster (*opposite*), he gladly accepted.

be taken back to a time that he fondly imagined to be more peaceful, less commercialised and full of good music. It was a time "when the world made more sense" and "you didn't have no worries".

The inclusion of the hymns "Just a Closer Walk with Thee" and "Be Thou My Vision" again gave the album a Christian tinge although, as ever, it was far from clear exactly what Van believed in.

It was even less clear whether Van felt he had achieved his longed-for union with God, or whether he was still hankering after it. At times he sang as though he was at play in the fields of the Lord, and at others he sounded hopelessly lost, as though he was doomed for ever to be pressing his nose against a stained-glass window.

At the end of 1991 the Belfast Blues Appreciation Society attached a plaque to the wall of 125 Hyndford Street, where it was unveiled on 26th November by legendary blues guitarist Buddy Guy. It read "Singer-songwriter Van Morrison lived here from 1945 to 1961". Although Van was due to play at the Belfast Opera House two days later he didn't bother to turn up for the ceremony, and was later reported to disapprove of being remembered in such a way.

He was further honoured in July 1992 when the University of Ulster awarded him an honorary doctorate of letters. Professor Peter Roebuc, Dean of the Faculty of Humanities, said in his citation: "As with the best singers and musicians there is an unremitting integrity in his work and a refusal to admit commercial compromise which, I suspect, has its roots – like his music – in the Ulster soil from which he springs.

"It has long been fashionable to accuse universities of remoteness from the communities which it is their duty to serve. In our case there could be no better answer to that charge, than our recognition of the excellence of one of our most celebrated local artists."

With that, the boy who had always been a loner and whose parents had worried what would become of him, walked forward in his red silk gown and his gold tasselled cap and accepted his doctorate.

Left: On stage in Gothenburg, Sweden, in 1990.

CHAPTER TEN

'TIL WE GET THE HEALING DONE

Twenty-five years after *Astral Weeks*, Van Morrison's position as an influential singer-songwriter is assured. He has created one of the most critically acclaimed albums of the rock era, has inspired another generation of musicians (Bono of U2, Elvis Costello and Bruce Springsteen, to name but three) and is still working as hard as ever both in the studio and on the road.

Shortly before the release of *The Best of Van Morrison Volume Two* in 1993, *Rolling Stone* magazine referred to him as "simply one of the greatest singer-songwriters alive". In January of the same year he had been inducted into the Rock and Roll Hall of Fame. Characteristically he hadn't attended the ceremony but had sent a faxed note of acceptance. His citation was read out by his old hero Robbie Robertson, formerly of The Band.

His distrust of the media is such that in 1974 a 74-page book *Reliable Sources* was issued to journalists in the hope that this would replace the need for interviews. "Caledonia Productions has produced this book to get out information that is as 'true' as possible," the introduction explains. "The music, of course, is its own statement."

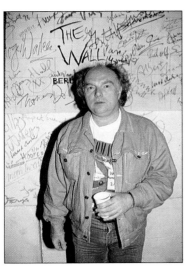

As a singer Van's natural talent is in the expressive quality of his voice – the unexpected blackness of the sound that emanates from this small Ulsterman – and also in his phrasing. The poetry he creates is not to do with the order of the words on the page but arises from his skill in exploring resonances. And his accomplishments as a band leader and arranger are often overlooked because of the attention that is focused on his latest statement.

Almost as important as his musical ability has been his artistic integrity. His audience trusts him because they believe that he writes and performs from the heart and that his product is not tampered with by record company executives.

His legendary "difficult" behaviour could be seen as Van's stand for artistic purity in the face of demands from the evil world of commerce. His grumpiness would then be not rudeness but a refusal to play the star game. Certainly he has made a brave attempt not to compromise his vision. From his point of view the problem comes not from his side – he is, after all, delivering the music – but from the predators who would strip him of his personal life.

By the record company executives, journalists, promoters, agents and publicists who require more of him than his songs, he is regarded as a nightmare. In his contract with Polydor Records, for example, there is a clause forbidding them to send out publicity photographs. On at least two occasions when magazine photographers have arrived for a session with him, he has told them that they are allowed to take one frame only. In 1983 *NME* reporter Gavin Martin was told that he could interview Van as long as he asked no questions about "the past".

Those favourably disposed towards the artist could see all this as an indication of his deep spirituality. They could argue that it is his extreme humility that causes him to avoid the glamorising tendencies of the camera. Recognising that he is a mere human, he is resisting all attempts to turn him into an idol. Likewise his brusque manner with journalists is his way of avoiding being burdened with sainthood. His mission is to go out into all the world and spread music. Anything else is a distraction. As he told *NME* journalist Tony Stewart in a notorious 1979 interview, "It's very hard for me to relate to people asking questions that are not only boring but don't have anything to do with my life or aren't relevant. It's a waste of time on my part because it drains me from doing what I really want to do, which is just to play music."

With the same evidence before them, those not so favourably disposed could see Van's behaviour as an example of inconsistent living. Here is this man, they might say, who is always singing about the joys of living with the Lord, yet who finds it hard even to raise a smile. Here is a man who rattles on about the need for healing, but who clearly lacks his own set of personal graces. Couldn't he stick unswervingly to his personal vision and yet do it all in a spirit of love, joy and peace?

Those who have worked with him closely speak of him as someone who seems to be permanently in some form of pain. One former band member describes his mood swings as being from "inner torture to less pain". It would make sense to see his spiritual quest as, in part, a search for something to rid him of this pain. It is significant that his most frequent yearning is to be "healed" and that Scientology, the one therapeutic technique that he has examined in depth, promises (according to L. Ron Hubbard) to remove "all psychoses, neuroses, compulsions and repressions".

Until he experiences this healing power, Van seems destined to be someone for whom spiritual cleansing exists as an ideal but who is prevented from carrying it through by unnamed personal demons. He is not being hypocritical when he sings of wanting to be lost in the love of God, but he is frustrated in his own personal search. "What he is trying to represent in his music is what he is like deep inside," says a former colleague. "But blocking the way is his pyschological self. There is no doubt that the insightful person in the songs is really there. But so is that aggressive and restless person."

The most common complaint from those who have worked with him, though, is not his temper but his apparent inability to communicate. The fear he has of revealing his deeper thoughts or his private life means that no one feels they have got to know him. Unfortunately this is coupled with a

For Van music is a serious business. Although it has brought him fame and wealth, his driving ambition has always been to explore his innermost soul and to use his gift to bring healing to himself and to his audience.

reluctance to indulge in small-talk, so that conversation is necessarily restricted to the subject of work.

After playing flute with Van around the time of *Astral Weeks*, John Payne concluded that all his personality had been absorbed into his voice and that there was nothing left to share with anyone else. "When he was on stage he would look like a space cadet but then he'd open his mouth and you would realise that he had channelled everything into the sound of his voice. The rest of it was just a shell that was there for the purpose of producing this noise."

Former road manager Stephen Pillster thinks that Van's "shell" has been built out of mistrust for almost everyone who comes into his life. "I've seen it in other musicians I've worked for who had their first success while they were still teenagers, and I've compared them with musicians who were 29 when they had their first hit. The difference is that the latter are the kind of people who have established their relationships, who have friends and next-door neighbours and maybe have a better handle on who is sincere and who is not. Van always starts with his guard up. He always wonders what someone wants from him, what their angle is."

Offstage he has a reputation for being sullen and uncommunicative, but in concert (*right*, drawn by Simon Jennings at the London Forum, May 1993) he comes alive.

Van Morrison's most recent album is *Too Long in Exile*, a 15-track offering of blues and jazz which confirms the pain and bitterness he still feels.

"Bigtime Operators" is a clear reference to Bang Records, whom he accuses of bugging his phone, getting him blacklisted and having him framed for drug possession. That the discontent he experienced in 1967 still bothers him so much is evidence of the unresolved conflicts he harbours. The title track, "Too Long in Exile", is a gentle moan about being away from Ireland (like James Joyce and footballer George Best), while "Wasted Years" is about being made a fool of and taking the "wrong advice". The spiritual hope is woven in with songs like "In the Forest" and "Til We Get the Healing Done" which echo the earlier songs "In the Garden" (1986) and "And the Healing Has Begun" (1979).

There is a slight feeling of disappointment with *Too Long in Exile*, in that Van seems now to be repeating himself both musically and lyrically – to be stuck in a groove of his own making from which he is either unwilling or unable to move on. The limitations of his art form are known to frustrate him. He realises that he is basically recycling the same five or six songs, and is reconciled to the fact that not all the fruits of his studies can be contained in a musical format. This is why the possibility of producing books, poems and lectures still interests him.

It is ironic that a man who professes to hate rock'n'roll and to regard it as "spiritually damaging" is now considered to be one of the rock'n'roll greats. That this same man has made spiritual transformation his chosen topic in a medium better known for glorifying the "lusts of the flesh" only increases the sense of irony. His development of religion as a normal topic of discourse in popular song may turn out to be his most lasting contribution. Were this to be so, it would bring him more pleasure than being remembered as a pop celebrity or as the singer who was loved by hippies.

Van Morrison is a genuine outsider. He is the boy from the streets of East Belfast who still doesn't want to join in the game that everyone else is playing. "Someone once described me as a maverick and that's what I would say," he says. "I'm a maverick not by choice but by conviction."

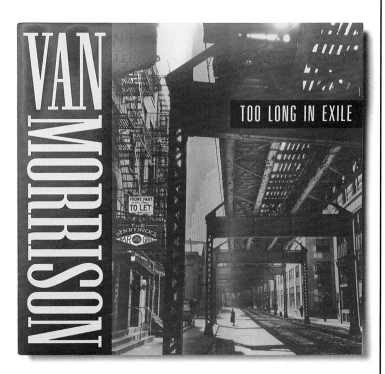

Although it was a marking-time rather than a breaking-through album, *Too Long in Exile* saw Van reunited with his blues hero John Lee Hooker (*opposite*). The album's reworking of "Gloria", with Hooker sharing the vocals, became a hit single in Britain in 1993. Van's first hit single, "Baby Please Don't Go", released almost thirty years before, had been copied from a Hooker record.

Alan Young 89.

DISCOGRAPHY

This list does not include compilations, re-releases, re-packages, bootlegs, spoken-word albums and oddities but concentrates on Van's main releases as a member of Them and as a solo artist. If an album or single reached the charts, its highest position is indicated immediately after the catalogue number.

Them Singles UK

Sept 1964 Don't Start Crying Now/One Two Brown Eyes (Decca F 11973)
Nov 1964 Baby Please Don't Go/Gloria (Decca F 12016) *10
Mar 1965 Here Comes the Night/All By Myself (Decca F 12094) *2
June 1965 One More Time/How Long Baby? (Decca F 12175)
Aug 1965 It Won't Hurt Half as Much/I'm Gonna Dress in Black (Decca F 12215)
Nov 1965 Mystic Eyes/If you and I Could Be as Two (Decca F 12281)
Mar 1966 Call My Name/Bring 'Em On In (Decca F 12355)
May 1966 Richard Cory /Don't You Know? (Decca F 12403)

Them Albums UK

June 1965 Them (Decca LK 4700)
Jan 1966 Them Again (Decca LK 4751)

Van Morrison Singles UK

July 1967 Brown-eyed Girl/Goodbye Baby (London HLZ 10150)
May 1970 Come Running/Crazy Love (Warner Bros WB 7383)
Dec 1970 Domino/Sweet Jannie (Warner Bros WB 7434)
June 1971 Blue Money/Call Me Up in Dreamland (Warner Bros WB 7462)
Nov 1971 Wild Night/When the Evening Sun Goes Down (Warner Bros WB 7518)
July 1972 Jackie Wilson Said/You've Got the Power (Warner Bros K 16210)
Aug 1973 Warm Love/I Will Be There (Warner Bros K 16299)
May 1974 Caledonia/What's Up Crazy Pup? (Warner Bros K 16392)
Nov 1974 Bulbs/Who Was That Masked Man? (Warner Bros K 16486)
May 1977 The Eternal Kansas City/Joyous Sound (Warner Bros K 16939)
July 1977 Joyous Sound/Mechanical Bliss (Warner Bros K 16986)
Nov 1978 Wavelength/Checkin' It Out (Warner Bros K 17254)
Feb 1979 Natalia/Lifetimes (Warner Bros K 17322)
Oct 1979 Bright Side of the Road/Rolling Hills (Mercury 6001 121) *63
Mar 1982 Cleaning Windows/It's All in the Game (Mercury MER 99)
June 1982 Scandinavia/Dweller on the Threshold (Mercury MER 132)
Feb 1983 Cry for Home/Summertime in England (live)/All Saints Day (12" Mercury MERX 132)
May 1983 Celtic Swing/Mr Thomas (Mercury MER 141)
May 1983 Celtic Swing/Mr Thomas/Rave On John Donne (12" Mercury MERX 141)
Oct 1984 A Sense of Wonder/Haunts of Ancient Peace (live) (Mercury MER 178)
Aug 1986 Got to Go Back/In the Garden (Mercury MER 231)
Aug 1987 Did Ye Get Healed?/Alan Watts Blues (Mercury MER 254)
Nov 1987 Someone Like You/Celtic Excavation (Mercury MER 258)

April 1988 Queen of the Slipstream/Spanish Steps (Mercury MER 261)
June 1988 I'll Tell Me Ma/Ta Mo Chleam Hnas Deanta (with Chieftains) (Mercury MER 262)
June 1989 Have I Told You Lately/Contacting My Angel/Listen to the Lion/Irish Heartbeat (Polydor VANS 1) *74
Nov 1989 Whenever God Shines His Light (with Cliff Richard)/I'd Like to Write Another Song (Polydor VANS 2) *20
Dec 1989 Orangefield/These Are the Days (Polydor VANS 3)
Jan 1990 Coney Island/Have I Told You Lately/A Sense of Wonder Spirit (Polydor VANS 4)
July 1990 Gloria/Rave on John Donne (Polydor VANS 5)
Sept 1990 Real Real Gone/Start All Over Again (Polydor VANS 6)
Nov 1990 In the Days Before Rock'n'Roll/I'd Like to Write Another Song/Coney Island (Polydor VANS 7)
Feb 1991 Enlightenment/Avalon of the Heart/Jackie Wilson Said (Polydor VANS 8)
May 1991 I Can't Stop Loving You (with the Chieftains)/All Saints Day (Polydor VANS 9)
Sept 1991 Why Must I Always Explain?/So Complicated (Polydor VANS 10)
May 1993 Gloria (with John Lee Hooker)/It Must Be You (live)/And the Healing Has Begun (live)/See Me Through (live) (Polydor VANS 11) *31
May 1993 Gloria (with John Lee Hooker)/Whenever God Shines His Light (live)/It Fills You Up (live)/Star of the County Down (live) (Polydor VANS 11) *31

Van Morrison Albums UK

Feb 1968 Blowin' Your Mind (London HAZ 8346)
Sept 1969 Astral Weeks (Warner Bros WS 1768)
Mar 1970 Moondance (Warner Bros WS 1835) *32
Jan 1971 His Band and the Street Choir (Warner Bros WS 1884)
May 1971 The Best of Van Morrison (President PTLS 1045)
Nov 1971 Tupelo Honey (Warner Bros K 46114)
Aug 1972 St Dominic's Preview (Warner Bros K 46242)
July 1973 Hard Nose the Highway (Warner Bros K 46242) *22
Feb 1974 It's Too Late to Stop Now (Warner Bros K 86007)
Oct 1974 Veedon Fleece (Warner Bros K 56068) *41
Mar 1977 A Period of Transition (Warner Bros K 56526) *23
Oct 1978 Wavelength (Warner Bros K 56526) *27
Aug 1979 Into the Music (Mercury 9102 852) *21
Sept 1980 Common One (Mercury 6302 021) *53
Feb 1982 Beautiful Vision (Mercury 6302 122) *31
Mar 1983 Inarticulate Speech of the Heart (Mercury MERL 16) *41
Feb 1984 Live at the Grand Opera House Belfast (Mercury MERK 36) *47
Feb 1985 A Sense of Wonder (Mercury MERH 54) *25
July 1986 No Guru, No Method, No Teacher (Mercury MERH 94) *27
Sept 1987 Poetic Champions Compose (Mercury MERH 110) *26
June 1988 Irish Heartbeat (Mercury MERH 124)
June 1989 Avalon Sunset (Polydor 839262)
Sept 1990 Enlightenment (Polydor 847100)
Feb 1990 The Best of Van Morrison (Polydor 841970)
Sept 1991 Hymns to the Silence (Polydor 849026)
Feb 1993 Best of Van Morrison Volume 2 (Polydor 517760)
May 1993 Too Long in Exile (Polydor 519219)

Them Singles USA

Don't Start Crying Now/One Two Brown Eyes (Parrot 9704)
Gloria/Baby, Please Don't Go (Parrot 9727) *93
Here Comes the Night/All By Myself (Parrot 9749) *24

I'm Gonna Dress in Black/Half as Much (Parrot 9784)
Mystic Eyes/If You and I could Be as Two (Parrot 9796) *33
Call My Name/Bring 'Em On In (Parrot 9819)
Richard Cory/Don't You Know (Parrot 3003)

Them Albums USA

Them (Parrot PAS 61005) *54
Them Again (Parrot PAS 71008) *138

Van Morrison Singles USA

1967 Brown-eyed Girl/Goodbye Baby (Bang 545) *10
1967 Ro Ro Rosey/Chick-A-Boom (Bang 552)
1970 Come Running/Crazy Love (Warner Bros WB 7383)
1970 Domino/Sweet Jannie (Warner Bros WB 7434) *9
1971 Blue Money/Sweet Thing (Warner Bros WB 7462)
1971 Call Me Up in Dreamland/Street Choir (Warner Bros WB 7488)
1971 Wild Night/When That Evening Sun Goes Down (Warner Bros WB 7518) *28
1972 Tupelo Honey/Starting a New Life (Warner Bros WB 7543) *47
1972 Like a Cannonball/Old Old Woodstock (Warner Bros WB 7573)
1972 Jackie Wilson Said/You've Got the Power (Warner Bros WB 7616)
1972 Redwood Tree/St Dominic's Preview (Warner Bros WB 7638)
1972 Gypsy/St Dominic's Preview (Warner Bros WB 7665)
1973 Warm Love/I Will Be There (Warner Bros WB 7706)
1973 Green/Wild Children (Warner Bros WB 7744)
1973 Ain't Nothing You Can Do/Wild Children (Warner Bros WB 7797)
1974 Bulbs/Cul de Sac (Warner Bros WB 8029)
1977 Joyous Sound/Mechanical Bliss (Warner Bros WB 8411)
1977 Moondance/Cold Wind in August (Warner Bros WB 8450) *92
1976 Wavelength/Checkin' It Out (Warner Bros WB 8660) *42
1979 Natalia/Lifetimes (Warner Bros WB 8743)
1979 Kingdom Hall/Checkin' It Out (Warner Bros WB 8805)
1979 Bright Side of the Road/Rolling Hills (Warner Bros WB 49086)
1979 Full Force Gale/You Make Me Feel So Free (Warner Bros WB 49162)
1982 Cleaning Windows/Scandinavia (Warner Bros WB 50031)
1984 A Sense of Wonder/Haunts of Ancient Peace (Warner Bros)

(Van Morrison left Warner Brothers in the summer of 1984 to join PolyGram which had been releasing his records outside America since 1979. PolyGram has discontinued the practice of releasing Van Morrison singles commercially in favour of CD singles for radio promotion purposes only.)

Van Morrison Albums USA

July 1967 Blowin' Your Mind (Bang BLPS 218) *182
Nov 1967 The Best of Van Morrison (Bang BLPS 222)
Nov 1968 Astral Weeks (Warner Bros WS 1768)
Feb 1970 Moondance (Warner Bros WS 1835) *29
Jan 1971 His Band and the Street Choir (Warner Bros WS 1884) *32
Nov 1971 Tupelo Honey (Warner Bros K 46114) *27
Aug 1972 St Dominic's Preview (Warner Bros K 46242) *15
July 1973 Hard Nose the Highway (Warner Bros K 46242) *27
Feb 1974 It's Too Late to Stop Now (Warner Bros K 86007) *53
Oct 1974 Veedon Fleece (Warner Bros K 56068) *53
Mar 1977 A Period of Transition (Warner Bros K 56526) *43
Oct 1978 Wavelength (Warner Bros K 56526) *28

Aug 1979 Into the Music (Mercury 9102 852) *43
Sept 1980 Common One (Mercury 6302 021) *73
Feb 1982 Beautiful Vision (Mercury 6302 122) *44
Mar 1983 Inarticulate Speech of the Heart (Mercury MERL 16) *116
Feb 1984 Live at the Grand Opera House Belfast (Mercury MERK 36)
Feb 1985 A Sense of Wonder (Mercury MERH 54) *61
July 1986 No Guru, No Method, No Teacher (Mercury MERH 94) *70
Sept 1987 Poetic Champions Compose (Mercruy MERH 110) *90
June 1988 Irish Heartbeat (Mercury MERH 124) *102
June 1989 Avalon Sunset (Polydor 839262) *91
Feb 1990 The Best of Van Morrison (Polydor 841970) *41
Sept 1990 Enlightenment (Polydor 847100) *62
Sept 1991 Hymns to the Silence (Polydor 849026) *99
Feb 1993 Best of Van Morrison Volume 2 (Polydor 517760) *176
May 1993 Too Long in Exile (Polydor 519219)

Select Bibliography

Van Morrison: Into the Music, Ritchie Yorke, Charisma Books, London 1975.

Van Morrison: A Portrait of the Artist, Johnny Rogan, Elm Tree Books, London 1984.

Van Morrison: The Mystic's Music, Howard A. DeWitt, Horizon Books, Freemont California 1983.

Van Morrison; Reliable Sources, ed. Cynthia Copple, Caledonia Productions, San Rafael 1973.

The Van Morrison Newsletter 1-9, ed. Stephen McGinn (available from 196 Duntocher Road, Clydebank G81 3NG, Scotland).

It's Too Late to Stop Now, Jon Landau, Straight Arrow Books, San Francisco 1972. (Review of *Tupelo Honey* by the *Rolling Stone* critic who went on to manage Bruce Springsteen.)

The Rolling Stone Interviews 1967-1980, ed. Peter Herbst, St Martin's Press, New York 1981. (Includes a 1970 Q&A interview conducted by folk musician Happy Traum.)

Psychotic Reactions and Carburetor Dung, Lester Bangs, ed. Greil Marcus, Heinemann, London 1988. (Stimulating re-review of *Astral Weeks* written by the late Cream critic in 1979.)

Off the Record, Joe Smith, Warner Books, New York 1988. (Contains a 1980s interview conducted by the author, who brought Van to Warners in 1968.)

The Rolling Stone Record Guide, Random House, New York 1979. (Dave Marsh reviews Van's album career from *Blowin' Your Mind* to *Wavelength*.)

The Rolling Stone Record Review Vol. II, Pocket Books, New York 1974. (Includes reviews of *St Dominic's Preview* by Stephen Holden and *His Band and the Street Choir* by Jon Landau.)

The U2 File, ed. Niall Stokes, Omnibus, London 1985. (Condensed version of a three-way conversation between U2's Bono, Bob Dylan and Van.)

The Rolling Stone Illustrated History of Rock'n'Roll, ed. Jim Miller, Random House, New York 1980. (Essay on Van by Greil "Mystery Train" Marcus.)

Written in My Soul, Bill Flanagan, Contemporary Books, Chicago 1990. (1984 *Musician* magazine interview by a particularly sympathetic and well-informed journalist.)

Riders on the Storm, John Densmore, Bloomsbury, London 1991. (Includes personal impressions of Them in LA during the summer of 1966 by former Doors musician.)

Picture Sources

Page 5: Redferns. Page 7, *clockwise from top left*: collection of Billy McAllen; collection of Billy McAllen; Michael Ochs Archives; David Gahr; collection of Andy Nieurzyla; Michael Putland/Retna; Adrian Boot/Retna; Rex Features; Michael Ochs Archives; Pictorial Press. Pages 8–9: John T. Davis. Page 10: Adrian Boot/Retna. Page 15: Hulton Deutsch. Page 16: Steve Turner Collection. Page 17: *top* collection of Billy McAllen; *bottom* Steve Turner Collection. Page 18: Steve Turner Collection. Page 19: *top & bottom* Steve Turner Collection. Page 20: *right* David Redfern/Redferns; *bottom left* Steve Turner Collection. Page 21: David Redfern/Redferns. Page 22: *top left* Gems/Redferns; *top right* Crixpix/Redferns; *bottom left* Glenn A. Baker/Redferns; *bottom right* Max Jones Files/Redferns. Page 23: William Gottlieb/Redferns. Page 24: *right* MJF/Redferns. Page 25: *top* William Gottlieb/Redferns; *bottom* Richie Howell/Redferns. Page 26: Atlantic Records. Page 27: Max Jones Files/Redferns. Pages 29–31: collection of Billy McAllen. Page 32: Pan Books. Page 33: *top* Gems/Redferns; *bottom* Bob Vincent/Redferns. Page 34: collection of Billy McAllen. Pages 35–6: collection of Roy Kane. Pages 39–40: collection of Pat Rossi. Page 42: Michael Ochs Collection. Page 43: Pictorial Press. Page 44: *top right* collection of Dougie Knight; *bottom right* Northern Ireland Tourist Board. Page 45: *Belfast Telegraph*. Page 46: Decca. Page 47: Michael Ochs Archives. Page 49: *top* London Features International. Page 50: Rex Features. Page 51: *top* Rex Features; *bottom* collection of Dougie Knight. Page 52: *inset* Michael Ochs Archives. Pages 52–3: Pictorial Press. Page 53: *top* Michael Ochs Archives. Page 54: Rex Features. Page 55: Michael Ochs Archives. Page 56: King Collection/Retna. Page 57: Rex Features. Page 58: Pictorial Press. Page 59: Michael Ochs Archives. Page 60: Rex Features. Pages 61–2: Michael Ochs Archives. Page 63: Fiona Simon/Retna Pictures. Page 64: collection of Jim Armstrong. Page 65: Michael Ochs Archives. Page 66: collection of Gary Trew. Pages 67–70: collection of Jim Armstrong. Page 71: *left* collection of Jim Armstrong; *right* Elliott Landy. Pages 72–3: collection of Jim Armstrong. Page 74: collection of Eric Bell. Page 75: Michael Ochs Archives. Page 77: *top* courtesy of Sony Records; *bottom* Elliott Landy. Page 78: *top* courtesy of Sony Music USA; *bottom* London Records/collection of Bob Kennedy. Page 79: Michael Ochs Archives. Page 80: *top* President; *bottom* courtesy of Sony Music USA. Page 81: *top* Michael Ochs Archives. Page 82: Don Paulsen/Michael Ochs Archives. Page 83: *left* Michael Ochs Archives; *right* Cezil McCartney. Pages 84–5: Michael Ochs Archives. Page 86: Warner Bros. Page 87: David Redfern/Redferns. Page 88: Clif Garboden. Page 89: Cezil McCartney. Page 90: Steve Turner Collection. Pages 91–2: David Gahr. Page 93: Steve Turner Collection. Pages 94–5: David Gahr. Pages 96–7: Elliott Landy. Page 98: Warner Bros. Pages 99–100: Elliott Landy. Page 101: David Gahr. Page 102: Warner Bros. Page 103: David Gahr. Page 104: Michael Putland/Michael Ochs Archives.

Page 105: David Gahr. Page 106: Elliott Landy. Page 107: Warner Bros. Pages 108–9: David Gahr. Page 110: Michael Dobo. Page 111: Warner Bros. Page 112: London Features International. Page 113: Michael Dobo. Page 114: Robert Ellis/Repfoto. Page 115: Warner Bros. Page 116: *left* Warner Bros; *right* London Features International. Page 117: Retna Pictures. Page 118: *top* Rex Features; *bottom left* London Features International; *bottom right* Andre Csillag/London Features International. Page 119: Robert Ellis/Repfoto. Pages 120–1: Rex Features. Page 122: Warner Bros. Page 123: *top* Rex Features; *centre* Michael Ochs Archives; *bottom* National Portrait Gallery. Pages 124–6: Barrie Wentzell/Repfoto. Page 127: *top & bottom left* David Gahr; *top & bottom right* Barrie Wentzell/Repfoto. Page 128: Richard Young/Rex Features. Page 129: Rex Features. Page 130: *top* Ian Dickson/Redferns; *bottom* Robert Ellis/Repfoto. Page 131: Barrie Wentzell/Repfoto. Page 132: Richard Young/Rex Features. Page 133: Rex Features. Page 135: Richard Young/London Features International. Page 136: BFI Stills, Posters & Design. Pages 137–8: Warner Bros. Page 139 Michael Ochs Archives. Page 140: Richard Young/London Features International. Page 141: collection of Andy Nieurzyla. Pages 143–4: Paul Slattery. Page 145: Mercury. Page 146: Mercury. Page 147: Adrian Boot/Retna. Page 148: Anastasia Pantsios/London Features International. Page 149: *top* Steve Turner Collection; *bottom* collection of Andy Nieurzyla. Page 150: Mercury. Page 151: Ebet Roberts/London Features International. Page 152: collection of Andy Nieurzyla. Pages 153–4: Mercury. Page 155: collection of Nancy Allen. Page 156: *left* Mercury; *right* collection of Andy Nieurzyla. Page 157–8: Paul Bell. Page 159: Adrian Boot/Retna. Page 160–1: Steve Turner Collection. Page 162: Mercury. Page 163: *top* Dick Barnatt/Redferns; *bottom* David Redfern/Redferns. Page 164: Polydor. Page 165 Paul Slattery. Page 166: Mike Garland. Page 167: Polydor. Page 168: Paul Slattery. Page 169: collection of Andy Nieurzyla. Page 170: Polydor. Page 171: Jeff Baynes/collection of Stephen McGinn. Pages 172–3: John T. Davis. Page 174: *middle Private Eye*; *bottom* collection of Andy Nieurzyla. Page 175: Kelvin Boyes/Pacemaker. Page 176: Cathal Dawson. Page 177: Michael Putland/Retna. Page 178: *top* collection of Bob Kennedy; *bottom left* Richard Young/Rex Features; *bottom right* Rex Features. Page 179: *top* Cathal Dawson; *bottom*: Andrew Catlin/London Features International. Page 180: *left* Chris Taylor/Retna. Page 181: Michael Putland/Retna. Page 182: Polydor. Page 183: Alan Young. Page 184: *top* Rex Features; *bottom* Paul Bell. Page 192: Michael Putland/Retna.